A New Paradigm of Education Rising

Guiding the Next Generations of Change-Makers in Holistic Education for the Soul, Body, Mind and Ascension

Published by: Motion Media International

Editors: Tiffany Oharo, Kit Brookman, Eric Wyman, Robert Janelle, Abyjane Richards, and Katie Beck.

Cover Design: Jeneen Gacek with gratitude to Mt Batur, Bali and *all* children.

Typesetting & Assembly: Motion Media International

Printing: Amazon

Creator: Monique Sayers - Primary Author

Title: *A New Paradigm of Education Rising-Guiding the Next Generations of Change-Makers in Holistic Education for the Soul, Body, Mind and Ascension*

ISBN Digital: 978-1-925919-51-6

ISBN Print: 978-1-925919-52-3

Categories: Education, Home Schooling

Dedication

"With gratitude to all children, teens, and change-makers, who are guiding us along the path of light towards *A New Paradigm of Education*. This includes our precious children: Coral, Ava, Charlotte, Noah, Matt, Josh, Ethan, James, Jessie, Java Jak, Khiana Kalli, Raffie, Amiya, Julian, Tatiana, Lorenzo, Eliana Rose, Jack, Alex, Oskar, Caitlin, and Connor. Thank you also to Mother Earth, our guides, soul families, and family members, including Mike, Trish, Shannon, and Tony. We love you all."

Acknowledgments for *A New Paradigm of Education Rising*

"Ida Rahayu is an innovative, passionate, earth-centric educator at one of the world's leading schools in education for sustainability, Green School Bali. Ida shares her passions for environmental regeneration, sustainable food, and entrepreneurship - through education - across a school community and beyond at a global level. Ida proves that education can be a mechanism of change for a sustainable future. What the world needs is more 'Ida Rahayu's."

~ Sal Gordon,
Head of Teaching and Learning, Green School Bali.

"Meka's story is a pillar of hope for her generation. Her life may look unusual from the outside, yet from within, she is living out her destiny by being the change the world needs. Meka's story has only just begun, and we can all learn something from her desire and drive to bring light and love to a dark world. To anyone at any age, Meka Leach exists to inspire us to live and learn from a mindful place. Thank you, Meka, for being an example of what it looks like to follow the call from the Universe."

~ Sarah Boezio,
Licensed Massage Therapist, Libra in Balance LLC.

"Clare Ford is a heart-centered innovative educational leader. Her chapter enlightens readers about the importance of individualized, spiritual learning and the supports needed for modernized creative instruction. Clare understands that every learner has the ability to light up with a love for learning. She knows our traditional system is outdated and crumbling and that our learners will thrive in the new paradigm."

~ Evelyn Shaw Corley,
Founder and CEO, Thrive International Academy, International Speaker, Published Author, and Meta's 2022 Changemaker Award Recipient.

"Karen Goodson and Julie Ferris's chapter is a very interesting and fascinating piece, clearly channeled, giving us some insights into soul contracts, lessons and purpose. The metaphor of a journey can help children and parents understand the different stages of life (and how we navigate them) from a higher perspective. Beautiful illustrations too."

~ Claire Knight,
from Wheel of Life Coaching. Professional life coaching for adults and teenagers.

"Aitabé Fornés' chapter on Sensethinking pushes us to remember how to reconnect to our sixth sense—our superpower and a magical self-directed learning tool for seeking truth, guidance on issues we and others face in our lives, tuning into our purpose, and ultimately experiencing a joyous and liberatory life."

~ Chemay Morales-James,
Founder of <u>My Reflection Matters Village</u>.

"Jeneen Gacek's chapter will resonate with so many parents! Her dive into the Self Directed approach gives you the 'behind the scenes' look at a parent's journey of self awareness, struggle, letting go and self trust. Her personal journey is deeply reassuring and her Family Philosophy is a helpful guide as a foundation for learning. If you are looking for the first step into this method, the Family Values exercise is a MUST."

~ Jo Symes,
Founder of ProgressiveEducation.org, an inspiration hub for exploring alternatives to conventional methods in education.

"Arianna Fox's interesting article is an analysis of what the future holds for the potential of youth moving forward. It was quite the insight, especially for mompreneurs raising kidpreneurs like me. It's full of real life examples and positivity and will tickle the curiosity of kids and parents who want to try a new pathway to education so they too can discover their passion and purpose just like Arianna."

~ Sylvia Tam,
CEO of Beviva Foods.

"Sian Goodspeed provides a compelling vision for a new educational paradigm. Based on her many years as a teacher, learner and parent, she offers us a radical alternative to the current disconnected model of education into a way of learning that is much more holistic, relevant and joyful. Importantly, it is an approach without judgement that nurtures, enables and supports children and values their inherent ability to learn. Sian even questions whether we should reconsider schools and move towards something much more community based and purposeful, where children develop an understanding of how to live in harmony with one another and the world. It is so refreshing to read how Sian believes we could reimagine education and whilst there is plenty to consider in making her proposals a reality, she gives us clear guidance as to how we can make it happen."

~ Richard Dunne,
Founder of The Harmony Project

"Brittany Tackett brings awareness to an important and overdue realization: our current education paradigm is devastatingly imbalanced. Her HeartFirst model offers a holistic approach to education, where our hearts provide a compass for learning journeys both unique and universal. With heart at the center of learning, Brittany encourages us to ponder how enriching our education, and thus our lives, could truly be."

~ Cassidy Kate,
Homeschooling Mom and Artist.

"While parents may be asking if their children will learn enough as a Self-Directed Learner, Khiana Kalli Gacek speaks to something much more meaningful. Without saying it, but by being it, she is exemplifying the depth of self-reflection and self-knowing that is available when freed from the constraints of social pressures and curriculum found in school."

~ Darcy Kaltio,
Learning Consultant for Self-Directed Learners.

"As the conscious parent of a highly intuitive sensitive child and Intuitive Counsellor, I know all too well the challenges sensitive children face in navigating the world. Alisha Braché does a tremendous job in highlighting workable tools to assist in setting these extraordinary young ones up for greatness. Normalizing these tools and ideologies will be a benefit to all children, parents, and educators alike. Alisha's story is the first in what I hope are many, to bring this important topic to the educators, guides and caretakers of our highly sensitive intuitive children."

~ **Zahra,**
Guidance by Z.

"Heidi Conway is helping young people and their parents recognize the freedom and power of being a changemaker. Traditional schooling prepares you for a life of conformity, striving and material accumulation. These things often don't make adults happy, let alone children. Heidi is a changemaker in education and beyond. She gives all who work with her the courage and coaching to seek a joyous life, lived with purpose."

~ **Tanja Kovac,**
Writer, poet and women's rights and gender equity advocate.

"Danielle Hayes provides an insightful account of her journey from educator to therapist, with well-thought-out and very interesting ideas for supporting children. A thorough and detailed summary of the nervous system is presented, including its impact on children's behaviour and learning. The connection between the nervous system and behaviour and learning, and how educators can help children by considering this is highlighted. The inclusion of case studies and suggestions for assisting children are helpful, and it's written in a warm and caring tone. A captivating and compelling read!"

~ Tamar D. Black,
PhD, Educational and Developmental Psychologist and author, *ACT for Treating Children.*

"This book beautifully aligns with holistic education which includes the body, mind, emotions, and soul ascension. This is exactly how we can support our next generations to grow up with a higher consciousness. A new paradigm is a place of co-creation, grace and allowance. I love how Monique Sayers and her co-visionaries have allowed this mission to unfold as a gift for humanity. The new paradigm of schooling is 5D, which this book will ignite further ideas about what role we can all play in this New Earth."

~ Gaby Kowalski,
Mission, Ascension and Abundance Coach, Mentor, and Channel. Founder of *The Oneness Foundation and Magic School for Kids.*

Table of Contents

———·——◦⟨◦⟩◦——·———

CHAPTER TWELVE

The Dawning of a New Paradigm 209

By Sian Goodspeed

CHAPTER THIRTEEN

I Believe and Trust in Myself - Mindfulness Education .. 233

By: Meka Leach, Age 13

CHAPTER FOURTEEN

Holistic Education of the Earth, Body, Mind, Soul
and the Rise in Ascension 241

By Monique Sayers

Conclusion: Closing Ceremony 263

AUTHOR BIOGRAPHIES

"We are living through a time of great transition - and we all have an important part to play in this transformation.

We are the bridging generation.

There is no right way. No one set path. It is all possible.

The old is breaking down and the new is being birthed.

So many people are starting to wake up, to consider, review, and realize what we are moving towards.

We are now able to find other like-minded people, share ideas, projects, initiatives all around the world as a vision for *A New Paradigm of Education*."

~ Sian Goodspeed

Introduction

Opening Ceremony

The father sky opens softly as the striking sun peers through soft, angelic clouds down onto mother Gaia's warm forest floor. Oh, how deeply peaceful education is! The sound of birds chirping, a waterfall splashing, and children laughing joyfully are inviting us all to gather for an important meeting known as *A New Paradigm of Education Rising*.

We welcome into the ceremony our educators, parents, teens, mentors, and intuitive beings from across the world sharing their wisdom, resources, stories, and codes. Introducing: Ida (Green School), Meka (Teen: Mindfulness), Danielle (Calm Kids), Aitabé (Sense Thinking), Alisha (New Earth Children), Jeneen (Self-directed Education), Karen and Julie (Portal of Potential), Arianna (Teenpreneur), Clare (SwitchedON Academy), Brittany (Heart-First Education), Heidi (The Change-Maker Way), Sian (Harmony in Education), Khiana (Teen: Life Paint) and myself (Awakened Education). There are a plethora of genres within this book, interwoven by light from one message to the next.

When an infinite number of people hold a collective vision, a paradigm shift happens. As guardians of education, we can

1

choose to *rise* sovereignly. Only from a state of full presence will empowering changes happen, as the old ego shatters and leaves space for new opportunities. *This* is education. The Earth is multi-dimensionally evolving – metaphorically and physically – as we move from one paradigm to another. Likewise, humans are multi-dimensional beings biologically inherited or changing.

This book is a vortex of light, known as *A New Paradigm of Education Rising*. It is not a fixed model, dogma, or one-size-fits-all approach, but a living consciousness that evolves *with* us. It's a place where conscious leaders, children, educators, parents, and all other light-beings and change-makers connect together to create an interconnected web of change in the evolution of education. We invite you to consider your vision for a new paradigm of education.

As you know, education is *not* a subject. Rather, it is an inner knowing as expansive as a rainbow, full of different colors but coming together to form one archway in the sky. We will explore holistic education, an approach that encompasses education as an "experience" rather than set subjects that lead down only one path. It is not about choosing one aspect or another; instead, it's about finding a balance within education that encompasses all aspects of the whole child/person. You will find education that supports the physical body, mind (IQ), emotional body (EQ)، soul or energetic body (EnQ)[1], and ascension, known as "Rising," in unison with the rhythm of the Earth. We not saying to never read or do math but instead to imagine "life as school," and learn in an array of holistic and joyful ways. Gone are the days of being asked, "What do you want to be when you grow up?"

---

1   Carrrie Jeroslow, A New Paradigm of Education, 2021.

There are infinite opportunities available to us *right now*. So rather than choosing a model of schooling that no longer serves, how about leaping to a new one?

The future of education will not be reached by holding onto the broken systems of the past. Nor is the future of education something we have to wait for – the future is *right now*. Throughout history, many models, pedagogies, ceremonies, philosophies, and research studies have offered insight into teaching from different angles. They have provided much knowledge and wisdom for which I am grateful. However, did these models ever evolve? Are they still applicable? This book strips away perceived realities and focuses on creating education that evolves for the highest good of all and is a letting go of all that no longer serves us.

If you could consider education as a living being, like a small child, an animal, or even a flowing strand of DNA, what kind of energy would you give it? I would assume it could be love, service, truth, and kindness. Yet, this has not always been the reality! I have experienced this first-hand as an educator and mother. I'm almost certain that you will have a story that you remember about your education or the children/students that you may be supporting. We have heard thousands of stories and seen other timelines where trauma was attached to education. What if, instead, we could all make changes towards becoming the highest frequency? What an enlightening paradigm shift we would see. There are infinite options available. It's time to navigate the path for ourselves, our ancestors, and future generations of change-makers as we move together on the bridge of light known as *A New Paradigm of Education Rising.*

In Honor of You:

In our first book *A New Paradigm Education*, the vision was created out of an intention to serve our students, who are leading us into this new paradigm of education. In this book, *A New Paradigm of Education Rising*, the authors and I wish to acknowledge YOU for joining hands with us to rise into this paradigm shift together. Showing up as the greatest version of yourself is the ultimate service; it can take dedication and a lot of learning (and unlearning). Thank you deeply. I feel your awakened heart ready to soar higher as we move along the golden bridge of light into the higher dimensions where new and ancient ways of learning are re-activated and remembered.

As we continue our circle gathering with great joy and humbleness, I present *A New Paradigm of Education Rising*. May it educate you in new ways as you open your mind, body, and soul to receive what a paradigm shift in education means for you.

With Gratitude,

Monique

A Message from the Council of Light

A New Paradigm of Education Rising is designed to bring light, love, and creativity to all who connect with it. Everyone will receive what they need from this book. It is embedded with energies of so many light beings and their connections to other realms and timelines. Many beings have come together to bring the energies required to move the educational paradigm forward from its state of scarcity. Yes, it is time for this to be presented to the world.

The color gold represents education from heart to heart and platinum gold connects you to your higher self and us as a tribe. Yes! As you go higher and higher, you will reach the diamond crystalline aspects that are multi-dimensional. These energies are the key to the birthing of the new paradigm in this dimension that we find ourselves in at this time.

There are many different areas that need to be addressed when we talk about education. Education is about learning, teaching, and also embodying the changes you desire. This new way of *being* will be teaching from the heart, the soul, and through the Avatar self. It is up to us to role-model these aspects and bring forth great change. And so it is!

This is a transmission of light-language that we have co-created in a Quantum session alongside the council of light for *A New Paradigm of Education Rising*. Light Language is an ancient and futuristic form of communication that connects with the soul, rather than the logical mind, which is attached to comprehension.

We have intentionally included light-language to normalize it within education. It supports learning by moving our energy to a higher frequency and the brain to the Gamma state. Gamma waves are associated with increased memory recall, sensory perception, focus, processing speed, and creativity, which are necessary for expanded learning. It also activates holistic education, healing, connecting, and exploring the body, mind, and soul.

Light Language can be spoken, written, transmitted through binaural beats, danced, signed with the hands, or toned. In this example below, the message came as sound that we channeled, and Julie Ferris then drew as symbols. Karen Goodson then translated these codes back into English, which are written in the transcription above. Please note: It is not necessary to "understand" light-language or even have it translated; instead, open your heart and feel the energy being expressed.

"Thoughts not rooted in the wisdom of the body are easily biased and manipulated. An educational system that focuses on mental thought without teaching how to access the greater intelligence of your body leaves you and your children disempowered and vulnerable.

What if instead, you could teach children how to tap into their highest intelligence to create the world their hearts desire?"

~ Aitabé Fornés

CHAPTER ONE

A New Level of Thinking: Thinking With All of Your Senses

By: Aitabé Fornés, M.Ed.

"We cannot solve our problems with the same level of thinking that created them."

- Albert Einstein

What if?

What if you could teach your children or your students how to tap into their highest intelligence to create the world that their hearts desire?

What if they knew with complete confidence that they had the skills to transform any challenge they meet into a win-win-win solution, where individuals, community, and the Earth all thrive?

What if the key to their success had nothing to do with the latest technology or extensive training and education, but rather an inner "technology" held within each and every person? An inner capacity that transforms learning from effort to joy. That turns problem-solving into immersive play. That opens new creative horizons which extend beyond the limits of our current imagining. What if, when they turn on this part of themselves, they also empower the things they most desire: abundance, connection, creativity, intelligence, healing, ease, peace, joy, and love?

This is possible right now by reestablishing the natural communication between the mind and the body. This connection has been disrupted due to cultural conditioning and an outdated educational paradigm, but restoring it can be simple and fast, and the impact is profound. It happens when you and your children or students learn to *think with all of your senses.*

The Intention of This Chapter

We are living during a great shift in consciousness that is bringing with it a new paradigm of education and the need for skilled guides to walk people out of the old and into the new. **The goal of this chapter is to support you, a conscious parent, educator, or facilitator, to become a new paradigm facilitator by teaching you how to unlock the intelligence of your whole body.**

Do You See This Too?

Our old thinking habits are destroying us.

People are overwhelmed with information. We struggle to interpret and make meaning of the competing ideas that fill our heads. News outlets and social media algorithms produce a steady stream of messaging designed to target us based upon our belief systems and shape our thinking. Gone is any attempt at balanced, unbiased reporting. The emergence of terms like *post-truth*[2], *fake news*[3], and *alternative facts*[4] give expression to this problem.

Mental overwhelm is not the only consequence. Our bodies and emotions are also triggered, making us reactive and ungrounded. With truth unmoored from fact, divisive argument, censorship, and explosive emotions prevail. Politicized discussions on social media quickly devolve into angry and mean-spirited comment threads. In this climate, relationships with family, friends, and neighbors have become strained or broken.

Worse than the polarization is the lost opportunity. We have so thoroughly demonized each other that rather than building coalitions to solve the underlying problems, we direct our energy towards proving each other wrong, or we gather in segregated spaces designed to exclude the people with whom we disagree. This results in more conflict and fewer productive solutions.

If we were to look at the most significant changes over the past 20 or so years, it would be easy to blame social media and its algorithms for the state we are in. However, the algorithm is just the latest mechanism taking advantage of a more fundamental vulnerability.

The Real Problem and the Real Solution

What makes people so vulnerable to the influence of a polarizing media or any form of social, political, or religious influence? As parents and educators, what role do we have in the solution?

---

2   https://en.wikipedia.org/wiki/Post-truth
3   https://en.wikipedia.org/wiki/Fake_news
4   https://en.wikipedia.org/wiki/Alternative_facts

The division we experience outside of us is a reflection of the inner split between our body and mind. This is why we have been so susceptible to conflict with each other. Our mind and body have been conditioned to operate as two disconnected energy centers. Yet, they continually seek wholeness through the other. This is because your mind can only *make sense* of information by offering its thoughts to the body's wisdom for discernment, and your body needs the conscious awareness of the mind to *make meaning* of its emotions and inner senses.

We are human beings; we are not just walking brains. Our ability to "make sense" is intimately bound to our senses. Mental processing alone cannot effectively discern between competing truths. We must be able to feel the truth in our bodies. We must also be able to tune into the constant flow of subtle perception that runs through our bodies like an underground river and cultivate the ability to draw this knowledge into our conscious awareness. Our role as parents and educators is to stop teaching our children and students that thinking is a mental process alone and teach them how to think with all of their senses.

Einstein said, "We cannot solve our problems with the same level of thinking that created them." I believe Sensethinking is a new level of thinking that allows us to solve entrenched problems.

My Promise to You

In this chapter, you will learn the three lessons that shifted me out of old ways of thinking and into Sensethinking. This will give you the foundation to become a new paradigm guide for the learners you support.

Who Am I?

My name is Aitabé. I'm an educator, a Family and Systemic Constellations facilitator, and the creator of Sensethinking.

Ten years ago, I was a high school teacher in New York City. For most of my career, I taught at a vibrant public school. The school was organized into small, interdisciplinary teams, and it encouraged and protected teacher creativity. In this environment, I taught science while incorporating mindfulness practices and systems thinking.

I thought of my work as three interconnected pieces, each supporting the other: the content and skills I was responsible for teaching, mindfulness practices, and systems thinking. Why these three elements? The choice was more intuitive than strategic. I wanted to be the best teacher I could be and serve my students as science learners and as life-long learners. I knew from experience that mindfulness practice creates holistic support for every part of a person's life, so I understood that, even if it did not directly teach them the content and skills of science, it would support their learning. That being said, I also designed creative ways to incorporate mindfulness practices into science teaching, such as through mindful observational drawing of nature during our study of plant evolution.

I also knew systems thinking was an essential concept for any scientific study. All things are interconnected, and life science, my subject area, provided the perfect way to teach this. I knew that my students would have the best grasp of the skills and content I was teaching if they could recognize the interconnected relationships between the parts of a system.

I had great success with this three-part teaching approach, so I was unfazed when I was required to work in a new school upon returning to teaching after an extended maternity leave. My new school had the same philosophy and design as my former school, plus I was an experienced and creative teacher who loved my work. I assumed I could transfer my previous approach to the new school with similar results. You can probably guess where this is going: it did not work out as I had imagined.

There's an expression in education, "*Maslow before Bloom*."[5] It's educational jargon used to convey the idea that learners must have their basic life needs met (as per the teachings of Abraham Maslow) before they can direct their attention to educational objectives (as described by Benjamin Bloom). In my new school, many students lived with such high stress that they couldn't focus on school. Their basic life needs were unmet, including the need for safety. Even with the skill, creativity, and care I had as a teacher, I was at a loss for how to serve them. Their needs required something that the school was unable to provide.

Yet, during this period, I had an experience that suggested a new educational possibility. It was not related to teaching, though. It was my introduction to Family and Systemic Constellations. Here's the story.

The Healing Modality That Changed How I Teach

January 2012

---

5   Abraham Maslow (1908-1970), a psychologist known for his "Hierarchy of Needs"; Benjamin Bloom (1913-1999), a psychologist known for his "Taxonomy of Educational Objectives."

I showed up at the Family Constellations workshop with butterflies in my stomach and a heaviness in my chest.

The butterflies were excitement, but the reason for the heaviness was less clear to me.

I had done a little research, so I had a general idea of what to expect: we would be chosen to represent members of a person's family system. However, this basic description revealed nothing of the multidimensional landscape I was about to experience.

A client took the chair next to the facilitator. He described his issue. He had a confusing relationship with his mentor, a man he greatly admired. Their visits would begin well, but as the visit would close, they invariably found themselves in conflict. He wanted to understand what was happening. They were supposed to be writing a book together but weren't making progress.

The facilitator asked him to set up a representative for himself and his mentor. The man looked around the circle of workshop participants. He chose one man to represent his mentor and another to represent himself. He walked each of them to the center of the circle and placed them facing each other about six feet apart. The two representatives stood silently in the center of the room, looking down. They both described themselves as feeling wobbly and unsteady.

The facilitator silently observed the representatives then turned to the client and asked him to set up a second representative for himself and his mentor. He placed the "second mentor" to the right of the first. He chose me as his second representative for himself. I stood across from the "second mentor."

Having never done this before, I was nervous and uncertain. What was I supposed to do? What if I did it wrong? I couldn't remember the facilitator's specific instructions. Maybe he didn't give me any instructions at all. Finally, he asked, "What do you notice?"

What I noticed was that my limbs felt weak. I felt that, if I didn't lie down, I would fall. I told this to the facilitator, and he instructed me to follow my movement. As I lay face down on the ground, my whole body felt cold, and I started shivering. Then, I experienced an unusual pressure where my body touched the floor, as if a magnet were pulling me to the ground.

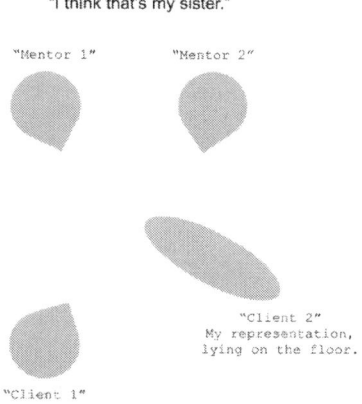

"I think that's my sister."

"Mentor 1"   "Mentor 2"

"Client 2"
My representation,
lying on the floor.

"Client 1"

"Who is that?" the facilitator asked as he extended his hand toward me. The client looked at me on the floor and took a deep breath. "I think that's my sister. She died as a child. I was six, and she was nine. My parents, in their grief, just packed up the house and we moved to another city. We never spoke of her again."

With the mention of his sister, I felt myself lighten. The warmth returned to my body. I looked up at him with a sense of playfulness and happiness that "I" was being spoken of in a positive light.

As the process continued, the facilitator asked me to stand. When I stood, I made eye contact with the man chosen as "the second mentor." Looking at him, I was overcome with emotion – so much love! Clear, radiant love. The facilitator said, "This is your father."

The facilitator invited us to follow our movements, and "my father" and I embraced. It was our longed-for reunion.

I returned to my seat in silence and awe. I felt like I was vibrating with energy. The heaviness in my chest that I had arrived with was replaced with warmth and lightness.

The Three Lessons I Learned from Family Constellations

I was profoundly affected by this experience. Here are the three things that stood out for me as an educator.

First, we didn't talk. We didn't address the client's question with any form of discussion, analysis, research, etc., in other words, none of the practices I taught in school. We received little information beyond the client's basic description of his issue. Instead of ordinary thinking, we used our bodies and represented different parts of the system then were invited to *trust our feelings* and report what we sensed. The information that came into my awareness when I represented the role I had been selected for arose spontaneously and was directly relevant to the client's question.

Further, it revealed an entanglement that the client himself was unaware of. Never had I been introduced even to the possibility that people could do this, much less the experience of it. It completely disrupted what I thought I knew about the nature of learning and information. "Wait a minute," I thought, "if this is possible, what else is possible?"

Second, where did this felt sense of peace and ease come from? When the process came to a close, the profound sense of peace I experienced was something I would experience after meditation, but even then, it was rare. More typically, it would require a whole retreat environment and no distractions. Yet, with no preparation, meditation, or special training, I had that same feeling of expansive peace, and it happened a few times that day! The shared experience also created a deep sense of connection with the other participants, people who were strangers just hours before. I thought about my students at school, who struggled to feel enough peace and harmony to sit with their classmates for even a few minutes. Could I bring *this* experience to the classroom?

Third, I could *feel* the difference between healthy and unhealthy, discordant and harmonious. I participated in a total of three sessions that day. Each time, I felt a shift in my body from confusion or tension at the beginning of the process to ease, expansion, and connection at the end. I was learning that the felt sense of peace, joy, or love was an indicator of systemic health and well-being. In contrast, confusion, tension, or other discordant feelings indicated a stuck, unhealthy system.

Here are the three key lessons I learned in that very first workshop:

1. You and I can access information directly through our bodies and senses, and this capacity can be used to answer the questions we care about.

2. Engaging our body and senses naturally nourishes our relationship with ourselves and our connection to others.

3. The health of a system has an energetic signature that can be perceived by the body and the senses. Positive, energized feelings reflect harmony and health, while discordant, low-energy feelings reflect stuck or unhealthy energy flows.

I left that workshop determined to learn more. By the following September, I had resigned from teaching and started training in Family Constellations. Alongside developing my skills as a Constellations facilitator, I independently developed tools to translate my new skills to education.

The Birth of Sensethinking

My teaching has been transformed by what I have learned over the past decade as a Family Constellations facilitator. To share what I have learned with others, I developed *Sensethinking*, a process designed specifically for education.

Here are the three main ways Sensethinking differs from Family Constellations:

1. Sensethinking is an inquiry process, not a healing modality

Family Constellations work is used for personal healing. Sensethinking is an educational practice designed for research and inquiry.

2. **Sensethinking does not require extensive training to learn**

   Training in Family Constellations typically requires a minimum of two years and hundreds of hours to become a confident, skilled facilitator. The basic practices of Sensethinking can be learned in a weekend and applied immediately.

3. **Sensethinking can be peer-led**

   Because each healing session is unique and must be attuned to the individual client, a Family Constellations session is facilitator-dependent. Sensethinking, on the other hand, is designed based on a pattern of inquiry that I came to identify after experiencing numerous constellations, a cyclical process I have named The Five Dimensions of Inquiry. The cycle guides the process, making it less facilitator-dependent and enabling peers to run it.

The discoveries my students make with Sensethinking astound me. In a short time, learners can dive deep into their questions, gain profound insight, and have a powerful interpersonal experience. With each inquiry, they increase their Sensethinking skill, becoming more intuitive and perceptive of hidden dynamics in a system. I sometimes refer to this as becoming the "smartest person in the room" because their development of systemic perception allows them to see what is unnoticed and inaccessible with ordinary thinking.

Here's a great example from one of my first workshops for teachers. Before you read, please note that the subject involves a racial slur and the history of slavery.

November 2015

Note: The "N-word" is spoken as written. It is a term used to refer to an offensive racial epithet.

"I want to know why my students use the N-word with each other. Don't they understand the history of that word?"

The questioner was an older African-American teacher from the Bronx. "I grew up in Virginia," he said. "I would never think of using that word."

I was surprised by the question. I was facilitating a professional development workshop for faculty and staff at a progressive public school in the Bronx, NY, teaching Sensethinking to a mostly Latinx and African American community. I expected the teachers to present something from their curriculum, not a personal, contemporary issue, especially one so charged. Immediately, I noticed bodies shifting in preparation for the discussion.

I reminded everyone that our work this day was not to use our analytic capacity but our *relational* intelligence to explore this question.

"Every question contains a system of relationships. What are the core relationships in this system?" I asked. After a brief discussion, we decided upon three elements, "Black Person," "White Person," and "The N-Word," and that they needed to be examined in two different settings: 19th-century slavery and 21st-century youth.

I asked for three volunteers, one for each element. The representatives for "Black Person," "White Person," and "N-Word" stood facing each other in the center of the room.

I told them that they were in the 19th-century slavery setting. After a few moments of silence, I invited them to follow their movement. Very quickly, "Black Person" moved across the room, as far away from "White Person" and "N-Word" as possible. At the same time, "White Person" and "N-Word" moved closer. "Black Person," now standing near the door, reported that he would leave the room if he could. "White Person" and "N-Word" stood shoulder to shoulder, looking silently at "Black Person."

"Why do my students use the N-Word with each other?"
Context: 19th Century Slavery

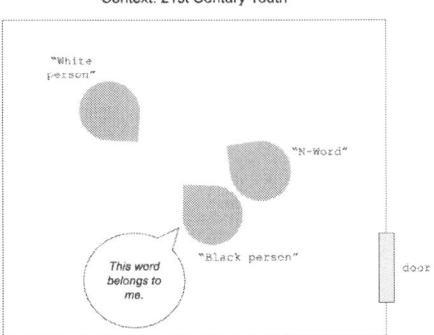

"Why do my students use the N-Word with each other?"
Context: 21st Century Youth

In the next round, I asked for three new volunteers. They represented the same elements, only now in the 21st-century youth setting. The representatives started as before, standing in the center of the room facing each other, but this time, "Black Person" pulled "N-Word" close and placed their right arm around "N-Word" while holding up their left hand as if to stop or block "White Person."

"White Person," said okay and took a step back. "Black Person" reported that they felt like "N-Word" belonged to them, and "N-Word" nodded in agreement.

We closed the exercise here. After thanking the volunteers, I asked the teacher who asked the question if he had any questions or reflections. He shook his head no. "I understand," he said.

Here's the new insight I gained from the experience: the relationship between the "N-word" and *ownership*. This was the fourth element in this system, and I could see that it came into existence in this systemic

23

relationship due to slavery. If we had represented "Ownership," it would be standing with "White Person" and "N-word" in the first scene. In the 21st century scene, "Ownership" would be standing with "Black Person" and "N-word." When the representative for Black people says that the N-word *belongs* to him, he is expressing, "You don't own this word, and you don't own me."

At the end of the workshop, a teacher walked up to me, looking very thoughtful. He had been the representative for "Black Person" in the second exercise. "This is revolutionary!" he exclaimed. "When we started, I couldn't imagine how we were going to answer this question without discussing it, but what we experienced, what we *felt*, was so revealing! This changes everything."

Sensethinking Reveals Hidden Dynamics

When I first started testing out these practices in education, I found the work compelling and engaging, but the question remained: would it really be more informative than just ordinary mental thinking? The answer is an unequivocal yes.

Take this N-word example. In an ordinary academic process, topics as sensitive as the history of racism and slavery can be very challenging. My experience has been that these discussions, if not sensitively facilitated, often end up with unresolved emotions that leave people feeling angry, hurt, and misunderstood. A bad experience can result in a decision to avoid the issue, especially with people they don't know well or who have different views. Understanding and reconciliation fail to occur, and the consequences ripple out into all of society.

With Sensethinking, on the other hand, we don't share our opinions. We don't debate, analyze, compare and contrast. Often, we barely use words. Yet, with this embodied, intuitive inquiry, we tap into a deep knowing. This allows profound new insight to arise directly from the process and leaves people deeply affected. Further more, the participants connect with each other. They get to experience their peers as channels of knowledge, not as opponents in an argument. Without a doubt, this is far more powerful than ordinary thinking.

My Desire for You: *Superpowerment!*

To review, here are the three lessons of Sensethinking:

1. You can access information directly through your body and senses rather than seeking answers outside of you.

2. Thinking with your senses nourishes your relationship with yourself and others, rather than depleting you from separation from the mind and body.

3. Truth and health are defined by the positive energetic signatures of a system and can be perceived by the body. Neither truth nor health result from having the "right" ideas in mind alone.

When I witness people turning on their Sensethinking, it's as if they are turning on their superpowers. And so, my wish for you is your own *superpowerment!*

You can have a taste of Sensethinking right now. On the next page, I will teach you one of my favorite Sensethinking exercises.

Resource: The Creative Forces Triangle

The triangle is a symbol of the forces of creation. It can represent mother, father, and child; thesis, antithesis, and synthesis; love, power, and creativity. Or, as in this example, the three points can represent the activating force, the restraining force, and the reconciling force. I teach The Creative Forces Triangle as one of the essential "maps" of Sensethinking.

The Three Creative Forces: Activating, Restraining, and Reconciling

The Three Creative Forces

Activating Force

Restraining Force

?

Reconciling Force

Activating Force: Need, desire, motivation, impulse. Anything that initiates the creative spark.

Restraining Force: The material or medium through which the activating force will take shape. This is not the same as an opposing force, though it may appear to take on that quality at times.

Reconciling Force: How will the partnership of the activating and restraining forces manifest? Through creative reconciliation. This is the energy that finds a way to bring together the activating and restraining influences to create something new.

Think of a clay pot. The activating force is expressed as the need for something to carry water. The restraining force is the clay that will be shaped into the vessel. The reconciling force is the creativity of the craftsperson. The clay pot is the manifestation of these three forces.

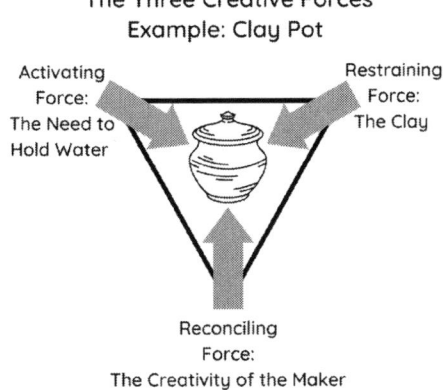

The Three Creative Forces
Example: Clay Pot

Activating
Force:
The Need to
Hold Water

Restraining
Force:
The Clay

Reconciling
Force:
The Creativity of the Maker

As archetypal forces of creation, everything that exists can be viewed through the lens of these forces. Sensethinking with the Creative Forces Triangle is a direct way to reveal the hidden dynamics shaping the issues you care about.

How to Use the Creative Forces Triangle for Sensethinking

Overview

The exercise is simple in concept. You bring a subject of inquiry to the triangle and use your body to sense how each force of the triangle feels in relation to your inquiry.

Choosing Your Inquiry

To begin, make a list of a few different topics you would like to explore. What can you choose? The possibilities are endless. A simple way to begin would be to select characters from a movie or book you enjoy and sense into the three forces for each character. You can choose a historical period you are interested in and identify people of events to investigate.

You can also choose something more personal, such as a challenge or issue that you are curious about. However, if you work with a personal topic, **do not do this exercise on *people in your life***; focus instead on the issue itself.

Why not use this about people in your life? Sensethinking is active sensing in a relational field. As a result, **consent is essential**. When it comes to working on personal relationships, there are additional specific considerations that I teach. For this exercise, if you want to work with people, choose characters from a book or movie or historical figures.

Set-Up

Write down the subject of inquiry plus each force on a sheet of paper, Activating, Restraining, and Reconciling. Place each sheet on the floor, creating a triangle. You will stand on the paper, so give yourself enough space between the sheets to stand on or over one sheet at a time.

You might wish to have a notebook/journal nearby to record your observations during the exercise.

The Exercise

Choose your subject of the inquiry. You may wish to write it down in your notebook. Once you have made the decision, you can relax your mind. You don't have to hold onto the subject with your mind in any way.

How to *Sense-Think*

Now it's time for the fun part! You will step onto each paper and feel the information in your body. This step might be challenging for your mind, but I assure you *your body will give you information*.

Step 1: Sensethinking Your Subject of Inquiry

Before you step onto the first paper, take a deep breath and soften your shoulders, neck, and belly, three areas where we often hold tension. Then step onto the center paper, Your Subject. Notice what it feels like to sense into this subject. I like to imagine that I have been placed in blindfolded in a room of treasures. Rest quietly and feel. Trust what arises.

Pay attention to any sensations, how your body wants to stand, and where you want to look or don't want to look. Notice how you relate to the other pieces of paper. Notice what thoughts arise. Welcome it all as information. If doubts arise, acknowledge them, but keep going. If you like, you can take notes about your experience.

Step off the paper and release all of the energy. You might want to shake or brush off your body to help you clear your mind and body. Bring your body to a neutral, relaxed state.

Step 2: Sensethinking the Activating Force

When you are ready, step onto the Activating Force paper. Sense as before. Feel free to change the location of the paper, if that feels right. Trust what arises.

When you complete this step, release the information and return to a neutral, relaxed state. Record any observations.

Step 3: Sensethinking the Restraining Force

When you are ready, step onto the Restraining Force paper. Sense. Change the location of the paper, if that feels right. Trust.

When you are complete, step off the paper and return to a neutral, relaxed state. Record your observations.

Step 4: Sensethinking the Creative Force

Step onto the Creative Force. Sense and adjust as needed.

As before, when you are complete, step off the paper. Brush off the energy or shake your body. Record any observations. You may wish to repeat the exercise a second time to check your experience or see if anything changed.

What if You Don't Feel Anything?

This is the most common concern I get. My response: Try again. Or try with a friend, where you each stand on different papers, or where one person stands as the subject and the other stands as the three forces. I assure you this is real, and it does work. Keep trying, and you will build your Sensethinking muscle.

Closing the Exercise

Before clearing away the papers, take a moment to be grateful for the new insights you received.

May this exercise serve you well and expand your capacity as a sense thinker. Blessings on your Sensethinking journey!

Aitabé Fornés, M.Ed. • www.sensethinking.com

"I cannot imagine anything more important than educating and nurturing the hearts of humanity. Not a single thing.

The New Paradigm of Education will help us bridge the gap between mind and heart and help people lead more conscious and fulfilling lives.

It only takes one generation of love to change the world."

~ Brittany Tackett

CHAPTER TWO

Imagine a World Where Hearts are Educated as Much as Minds

By: Brittany Tackett, MA

*"Educating the mind without educating the heart is
no education at all."*

- Aristotle

The old paradigm of education operates under a materialistic worldview, where "to have is to be" is creating a sense of lack because we can never have enough and are left always wanting more. As a homeschool mom, transpersonal psychologist, EQ coach, and yoga and meditation teacher, I see a new paradigm of education on the horizon, one that operates under a transpersonal worldview, where "to love is to be" and we are always enough because love is abundant and ever present in our hearts.

All through school, I was taught to chase the American Dream. I was told that success meant attending college, getting a 9-5 job, buying a house, getting married, and having children. I came from a long line of poverty and struggle. I was the first in my family to graduate high school, so education was important to me. Therefore, I chose to go to college no matter the cost, believing that it was the key to a better life.

I received scholarships, but it still wasn't enough to pay the high cost of tuition. So, without fully comprehending what I was getting myself into, I took out student loans. I had no idea that I was signing myself up for a potential lifetime of compounding debt.

I believed that college would bring me a sense of success and financial stability that my family never knew. It never occurred to me that one day in the future, I may not want to work 40 hours a week to pay back the loans. I never once thought about what motherhood would be like and that I would end up wanting to be a stay-at-home mother who homeschools her children.

I wasn't educated to seek purpose or meaning in life. It was never about finding what made my heart sing. It was about finding a career that would make a lot of money. I was always a star student who wanted to succeed in school. But, in many ways, my education failed me, and I had so much healing and unlearning to do as a result of it.

I had a spiritual awakening in my twenties, and my entire worldview crumbled beneath me. My heart was telling me to travel and see the world. It was calling me to live a slower life, learn to live off the land, and move to an off-grid lifestyle. But I realized then that I couldn't follow that dream because I had already enslaved myself with student loan debt, some of which my family had co-signed for me, which meant that, if I chose to leave the system and ignore the debt, then it would fall on their shoulders.

I began to feel paralyzed by the debt and experienced depression and anxiety because of it. I didn't know what to do with my life in the material realm, so I focused all my energy on my spiritual growth. I realized that many of the truths I had been handed in childhood didn't resonate. So, I began a path of self-education: studying every religion, philosophy, and spiritual practice I could find.

I came upon transpersonal psychology, and even though it was far outside the norm, I knew it was the path for me. Since I was already heavily in debt anyway, I trusted my heart and took out more loans to pursue a graduate degree in the field.

Transpersonal psychology differs from mainstream, behavioristic psychology. It is holistic and not only acknowledges the whole person but also goes beyond the person and looks at the spiritual dimension of humanity. During my graduate studies, I began to have a vision for a new paradigm of education and wrote a graduate paper on "Moving Towards a Transpersonal Education System."

A few years later, I was divinely guided to a position as a school-based mental health therapist position, a job I didn't think I was "qualified" for because I chose to pursue transpersonal psychology rather than going the clinical route and getting "licensed." Again, this shows that, when something is meant for you, life finds a way to make it happen, even when it falls outside the constraints of our systems.

I spent four school years in this position, working with more than 100 children and teens in the public school system. Through this work, I gained frontline experience of the blind spots in our educational paradigm. I observed a huge disparity, with so much emphasis on the thinking mind and very little on the feeling sense.

Elementary-aged students were taught math, science, and literature every day but were in counseling classes for only one hour every two weeks. Middle school and high school students were left virtually on their own. They could visit the guidance counselor if they needed help, but they no longer had formal social and emotional education.

As a therapist, I routinely worked with only those children who were exhibiting social, behavioral, or emotional problems or who had knowingly been through some sort of trauma. These kids started spontaneously referring to me as "The Feelings Teacher," and they came into sessions excited to share their feelings with me and learn skills to manage them in a healthy way.

I felt strongly that all students should be given emotional education and support and that it should be a part of their daily routine at school. I began to receive more downloads of a new education model. I started envisioning what our world could look like if hearts were educated as much as minds. I felt called to birth my business, HeartFirst Education, to help usher in the new paradigm and bring this vision to life.

Educating the Whole Person, HeartFirst

Martin Luther King Jr. wrote in *The Purpose of Education,* "The most dangerous criminal may be the man gifted with reason, but with no morals."

When we operate from the mind (as the old paradigm of education does), profit can become more important than people, opinions become more important than relationships, and progress becomes more important than sustainability. Therefore, we must balance education of the mind with an education of the heart, focusing on emotional intelligence and virtue development.

"I wish that one day, formal education will pay attention to the education of the heart, teaching love, compassion, justice, forgiveness, tolerance, and peace. This education is necessary, from kindergarten to secondary schools and universities. I mean social, emotional, and ethical learning. We need a worldwide initiative for educating heart and mind in this modern age."

-Dalai Lama

THE HEARTFIRST EDUCATION MODEL

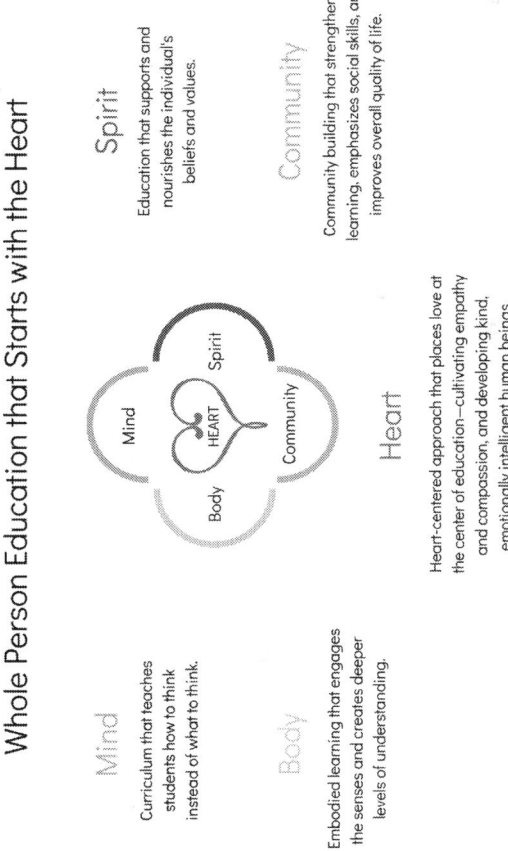

Whole Person Education that Starts with the Heart

Spirit
Education that supports and nourishes the individual's beliefs and values.

Community
Community building that strengthens learning, emphasizes social skills, and improves overall quality of life.

Mind
Curriculum that teaches students how to think instead of what to think.

Body
Embodied learning that engages the senses and creates deeper levels of understanding.

Heart
Heart-centered approach that places love at the center of education—cultivating empathy and compassion, and developing kind, emotionally intelligent human beings.

Traditional education models have separated the mind from the rest of the human experience. Learners mostly sit still and listen. Read, write, and repeat. But we are multidimensional beings. Focusing on educating, only one aspect of our existence creates an imbalanced society.

The HeartFirst Education model is holistic and focuses on educating the whole person, heart first. This model encompasses all aspects of the human experience: mind, body, spirit, heart, and community. The heart always comes first because nothing is more important, potent, or powerful than love and our ability to give and receive it through our hearts. Community is also included in the HeartFirst model because we are social beings who need each other to survive and thrive.

MIND

"The mind is a wonderful servant but a terrible master."

- Robin Sharma

The purpose of education is not simply to fill a person's head with facts, preconceived notions, or beliefs. Instead, true education encourages critical thinking, curiosity, and divergent thought. It's not so focused on memorizing answers, but rather on remaining open-minded enough to ask questions.

The current education system puts math, language, and other left-brain activities at the top and places art, music, and other right-brain activities at the bottom. Holistic education recognizes that both are equally valid.

While our old paradigm has focused so heavily on educating minds, it has focused little on understanding the power of thought, shifting your mindset, and learning how to control the mind rather than letting it control you.

I grew up identifying with my mind, not realizing the deeper "I am" presence that exists beyond thinking. My mind was trained to think negatively, and I never questioned the validity of my thoughts or realized that my victim mentality was limiting me.

It wasn't until my twenties that I discovered another way of being, learning mindfulness meditation and cognitive behavioral therapy techniques. These teachings changed my life. If I had learned them as a child, I could have made better choices and avoided unnecessary suffering.

The new paradigm will instill mindfulness from a young age. Rather than just telling children to pay attention and becoming frustrated when they can't focus, we will actually teach them how to pay attention through mindfulness skills. This involves teaching kids to be present in the moment, practice contemplation, develop self-awareness, and become the witness and observe their experience from a place of curiosity, nonattachment, compassion, and love.

Children will also be taught to notice the quality and tone of their thoughts. They will learn to recognize the difference between helpful and unhelpful thinking and to shift unhealthy thoughts into positive, healthy self-talk.

Our minds are incredibly powerful. Look at all that we have created that was originally just an idea in someone's mind. Take a moment and peer back into history and observe how mental constructs continuously change the course of life for humanity.

Look at all that humans have created with technology. It is extraordinary what we have accomplished. But unfortunately, our emotional evolution hasn't matched the pace of our mental expansion. So, you might say that, technically and intellectually, we are living in a golden age, while emotionally, we are still living in the stone age.

Our thoughts become things. When we think of an idea, we find a way to manifest it into reality. So, what if we collectively shift our focus to thoughts of a loving, unified society? What if we trained the mind to serve the heart and used our intellect and technology for the highest good?

BODY

Just as the old paradigm ignores the heart, it also ignores the body. Unfortunately, I learned through my schooling to do the same. I was the proverbial professor, who merely used her body to carry around her head. I didn't even realize how disembodied I was because I was so engrossed in my mind.

I didn't exercise or play any sports, as I associated both with traumatic experiences in gym class where a teacher berated me for not being able to run a mile, and I was laughed at by students when I couldn't dribble a ball down the court.

I started to hate my body. Not only did I feel uncoordinated, out of shape, and incapable, but I also felt ugly because other students constantly criticized how I looked. I learned through my schooling that it was safer to live in my mind, so I completely ignored my body.

I still remember how furious I felt when I learned that physical fitness classes were required for my undergraduate program. I thought it was a waste of time, that it had nothing to do with my psychology degree, and expected to gain nothing but shame from a fitness class. I'm happy to share now that my assumption was wrong.

A friend suggested we try yoga, which I knew nothing about. I reluctantly agreed, and it changed my life because it brought me back to my body. I was surprised that I didn't feel shame in yoga class. Instead, I felt a newfound sense of calm, ease, and flow.

As I deepened in my yoga practice, I realized that yoga helped me release old feelings, like anger and shame that had been repressed and stored in my body. So, it turned out that yoga actually had everything to do with my psychology degree, and there was much more to the mind-body connection than I had previously considered.

I loved yoga so much that I continued to practice regularly and eventually became a certified yoga instructor. I now teach several classes a week to children and adults. During my work in public schools, I introduced yoga to elementary students who were eager to move and explore their bodies in a more engaged and meaningful way.

Yoga is an excellent way to honor the body, enhance learning, and help children connect to their highest selves. Yoga means to yoke or unite. It serves as a bridge for mind, body, spirit, and heart. Yoga helps foster mindfulness, embodiment, and self-regulation, all important components of a holistic education model.

The body is the first educational system that we experience as human beings. We begin learning and exploring in and through the body while still in the womb. Children live in their bodies naturally but often learn through schooling to ignore the body and keep their awareness in their minds.

41

Many children are hands-on learners and need to experience their learning with their bodies to absorb it fully. So even something as simple as adding movement to fact memorization can go a long way (if we even need to memorize facts in the new paradigm.)

Holistic education engages the senses and allows children to embody their learning and experience it fully in the present moment. This means getting out in nature and connecting to the world around them. This also means connecting to their bodies and developing body awareness and interoception.

Another aspect of embodied learning is emotional intelligence or EQ. When we teach EQ, we teach children to pay attention to their bodies. We teach them to notice the physiological sensations that arise when they have an emotion. We also teach them to listen to their body as the authority. This means, when they feel hungry, they eat, and when they need to use the restroom, they go rather than wait for an outside authority to permit them to take care of themselves.

SPIRIT

We are spiritual beings having a human experience, and the new paradigm will reflect that understanding. Holistic education not only recognizes but also nourishes the spiritual dimension of our humanity.

The old paradigm says, "I know," while the new paradigm says, "I love."

The old paradigm says, "I have," while the new paradigm says, "I am."

It is not about what you do or what you have. It is about who you are and how you are being.

Within each of us is a light, a tremendous source of energy and power that, when used lovingly, can create extraordinary change in the world. The goal of holistic education is to help each human being awaken this power and use it for the highest good of all.

While the highest potential of a human being is unique to the person, it ultimately comes from living in a higher state of consciousness where we lead from a place of love. It is having a strong sense of meaning, purpose, and connection to source energy. It is shifting from "me consciousness" to "we consciousness" and recognizing that we are all one. There is no separation.

However, while we are all one, we are also original. To truly make a difference in the world, we must be different. Yet, the old paradigm of education promotes sameness and conformity, leading many people astray from their authentic selves as they try to be someone they're not.

The old paradigm of education is subject-centered. Our new paradigm of education will be person-centered. This means that education will look different for each person, and our differences will be celebrated rather than feared.

In the old paradigm, children are often asked the cliché question, "What do you want to be when you grow up?" This teaches them to associate their identity with a career and brings them out of the "here and now" and into thoughts about the future. This question will have no place in the new paradigm where we are focused on who we are and how we are being in the present moment.

COMMUNITY

Humanity is a social species. Our relationships are essential to who we are. Therefore, community will be a central value in the new paradigm of education. We will encourage cooperation and collaboration over competition. We will recognize that we can accomplish more when we work together, rather than working against each other.

When we truly learn to let go of individualism and all this focus on "I," "me," and "my" and start shifting our perspective to "we," "us," and "ours," there will be far more empathy in the world because humans will see beyond separation and recognize their brothers and sisters as parts of themselves.

The old paradigm drives separation. The new paradigm creates unity, teaching the concept of oneness by illustrating our innate connection to each other and all species on Mother Earth.

The new paradigm of education is not separate or distinct from nature. On the contrary, we recognize that we are all one and part of nature, not apart from nature. Therefore, nature education will be of utmost importance in the new paradigm.

Ideally, education will take place outdoors most of the time, in the open air, whenever the weather allows. Children will be taught to plant trees, garden, and build fires. Time will be given to engage fully and connect to animals and plant life, as well as time to saunter, rest in silence, and observe without interfering.

Think Outside the Building: The World is Your Classroom

Education doesn't need to be separated from the greater community. Children don't need to be pulled away from the family unit to learn. They don't require the school system to develop social relationships either.

I've found through my homeschooling experience that homeschoolers have more opportunities to develop deeper and richer relationships because families come together and learn as a collective, rather than separating children by age and educating them away from siblings and parents.

Education isn't confined to four walls. Humans don't need to sit in a building eight hours a day, five days a week, to get a "quality education." Learning is everywhere, every day. Life is school, and the world is our classroom.

In the new paradigm, we will see many different models of education. We will see some students educated in school settings, others at home, and some out in the world, whether from roaming the forest, swimming in the ocean, or traveling to another country.

HEART

"Having a smart brain is not enough; we also need a warm heart. So education must develop our intelligence and support the basic human values of warm-heartedness and compassion."

– Dalai Lama.

In ancient times, the heart was considered the center of consciousness, and the mind was merely an extension of it. However, in modern times, our society has focused heavily on the mind and ignored matters of the heart almost entirely.

We must ask ourselves: Are we thinking beings who feel or feeling beings who think? According to Doc Childre, founder of HeartMath institute, an organization dedicated to activating the hearts of humanity, "We evaluate everything emotionally as we perceive it. We think about it after."

Educating the whole person, heart first, means we consider the person's well-being first. It means emotional intelligence takes precedence over academic intelligence. EQ is more of a predictor of future success in one's career, relationships, health, and overall quality of life than IQ. Yet, our formal education systems spend so much time and energy educating the mind and, in doing so, neglect the heart.

We must put well-being first as the primary educational goal or benchmark. If someone feels anxious and their nervous system is in fight or flight mode, learning doesn't happen anyway because the prefrontal cortex is shut off, and the limbic system is running the show.

I envision an education where we ask, "What do you feel?" as often as we ask, "What do you think?" The new paradigm will encourage people to listen and follow their hearts, which often means following their joy. I firmly believe whatever brings you joy, you need more of that in your life.

We put so much emphasis on the mind, but it isn't who we truly are. Just think of the phrase "learn it by heart." We use this expression to mean that we have learned something and now know it from memory. The heart has a knowing that goes beyond the mind, and the new educational paradigm will teach us to trust that knowing.

The heart also trusts divine timing. We don't need to rush to deadlines or try to force learning to happen. It will happen organically. We must recognize that learning is not truly linear. It's more of a figure 8, with us circling back to things again and again throughout our lives.

The heart is our channel to the divine. It is where we experience love. When we live from our hearts, we operate from a deeper and higher place. Through the new educational paradigm, we will learn to feel safe in the heart's vulnerability and release the need to armor our hearts as a form of self-protection.

What's Love Got to Do With It?

"Love is the most powerful force in the universe and we have the extraordinary ability to give and receive it."

- Tim A. Ewell

If education aims to prepare our youth for life and help them reach their full potential, then how could love, the most powerful force within us, not be an integral part of it? Psychiatrist Viktor Frankl, while struggling to survive in a Nazi death camp, realized, "Love is the ultimate and highest goal to which one can aspire." Love is what gives meaning to our lives. It eases our suffering and connects us.

Imagine if we, as a collective, taught and learned from the lens of love. Imagine what our world would be like if love were the highest goal of education. Imagine what kind of society we could have if we were taught from a young age that love was the highest purpose, vision, intention, goal, and expectation for our lives.

How would this shift the outcome of education? How would this change the way we engaged with one another? With the greater community? How might it transform the way we see ourselves and others?

The mind-oriented paradigm is primarily driven by fear. But, while fear serves an essential evolutionary purpose, fear is the opposite of love. Fear is rooted in the mind. Love is rooted in the heart. Fear wants to make sure we survive. Love helps us thrive.

Fear contracts while love expands. Fear begets more fear. Love begets more love. Fear creates separation by wanting to protect itself, but love knows only unity.

Love is who we are. It is our true nature. Love is the highest vibration on this planet, and it encompasses all things. Love is the greatest force in existence and our most powerful asset as human beings.

Virtue Education

> *"If you have the chance to be exposed to a loving, understanding environment where the seed of compassion, loving-kindness, can be watered daily, then you become a more loving person."*

- Thich Nhat Hanh

We all have an incredible capacity for love, compassion, empathy, acceptance, tolerance, and forgiveness. These are some of the highest human virtues, and our education systems must reflect their importance in order for us to reach higher states of consciousness as a collective. If these inner values were our educational benchmarks and the heart was the central focus of education, imagine how that could change society.

When I worked in public schools, I was shocked to find out that few elementary students could define the words "empathy" or "compassion." Most of them told me that they had never even heard the words before.

Every child should know the words "empathy" and "compassion." They should hear these words regularly, understand their importance, and recognize that these virtues are skills they can develop and sharpen with practice. Every person has the innate ability to embody the highest virtues of the human heart, and holistic education can help foster the actualization of these virtues.

The Way Forward

I honestly cannot imagine anything more important than educating and nurturing the hearts of humanity. Not a single thing. This is truly the most valuable thing we can do with our time here.

The new education paradigm will help us bridge the gap between mind and heart and help people lead more conscious and fulfilling lives.

Human goodness is truly extraordinary. Goodness is God (spirit, source, whatever you choose to call it) manifesting itself through humanity. When we allow our goodness to shine through, we live our highest purpose and allow the divine to live through us.

What are our hearts capable of? Have we even scratched the surface? We've spent centuries educating minds and have seen what our minds can do. But, what about our hearts? What kind of world is possible if we, as a collective, let our hearts take the lead?

I experienced an incredible transformation when I stopped living in my head and started living from my heart. I'm happy to share that I no longer feel crippled by my student loans. I let go of the fear and boldly followed my heart, trusting entirely in my life's purpose and path. My heart has led me to a good place, where I can serve others in a way that nourishes rather than depletes me. I can pay my loan payments without having to work forty hours a week. Instead, I live freely, homeschooling my daughter and only taking on work that aligns with my authentic self.

The greatest difference you can make in the world is simply to live from your heart. Whatever you choose to do with your life, I encourage you to do it with love. When you live in love, your heart radiates love out to the hearts of others through the electromagnetic field, raising the collective consciousness of the entire planet.

It only takes one generation of love to change the world.

May your heart and the hearts of those around you be filled with love.

Resources

<u>Mind</u>

Mindfulness

Mindfulness is the practice of purposely paying attention to the present moment nonjudgmentally, with an attitude of friendly curiosity and kindness. It is directing your attention to what is actually happening NOW and looking at the present moment compassionately, allowing it to be precisely what it is.

We can make mindfulness more fun for kids by asking them to be superheroes and engage their "spidey senses" or use their "Jedi mind power" to explore the present moment.

Five Senses Exercise

Look around you and find:

- Five things you can see
- Four sounds you can hear
- Three things you can touch
- Two things you can smell
- One thing you can taste

You can make this more exciting by finding items to explore with their senses, such as feathers to touch, musical instruments to listen to, and fresh herbs to smell. Taking a slow, intentional walk in nature is also a great way to practice mindfulness.

Body

Body Scan

The body scan mindfulness practice is a great way to help children bring awareness to their bodies.

Start by lying down and closing your eyes. Then, bring your attention to your internal experience. Take three deep breaths, feel the rise and fall of the belly and chest, and observe how your body feels in the present moment.

Bring awareness to the feet. Feel the energy of the feet and notice what physical sensations are present. Next, begin moving up to the legs, scanning the ankles, shins, knees, and thighs and observing the sensations in each space. Continue up the body, slowly scanning the hip area, belly, back, and chest, followed by the arms, neck, and finally, the face and head.

There are many animated videos available on YouTube that will walk children through this process.

Spirit

Gamma Breath

Gamma waves are the fastest brain waves. They occur when we are highly conscious, alert, engaged, and in flow. Gamma waves are considered to be the ultimate brain state. They're associated with greater happiness, heightened creativity, enhanced memory, higher cognition, and improved problem-solving ability. Tibetan Monks show high levels of gamma waves, likely because of their consistent mediation practice.

The breathing practice below (Gamma breath) can help to stimulate gamma brain waves.

Inhale through the nose for a count of four. Next, exhale through the nose for a count of four. Next, inhale through the nose for a count of four. Then, exhale through the mouth for a count of four. Next, inhale through the mouth for a count of four. Next, exhale through the mouth for a count of four. Finally, inhale through the mouth for a count of four and exhale through the nose for a count of four.

Repeat this two more times.

Heart
Heart Coherence Breath

Researchers at the HeartMath institute have scientifically proven heart coherence breathing puts you in a coherent heart state where your brain and heart work in balance and your nervous system functions optimally. This is a calm, energized state where you feel a deeper connection to yourself and the world around you.

To practice heart coherence breath, simply inhale for a count of six and exhale for a count of six. This equates to just five breaths a minute. This slow, deep breathing helps to calm your nervous system and regulate your heart rhythm.

You can experiment with inhaling and exhaling through the nose or mouth. What is most important is the slow rhythm of the breath. Practicing heart-coherence breathing for at least three minutes is recommended to achieve a heart coherent state. But, naturally, the longer you practice, the more benefits you will likely notice. You can practice this breath in any position, but a seated position is recommended, as lying down changes the direction of the heart's current.

Community

HeartFirst Kids Network

HeartFirst Education has recently launched the world's first online social-emotional learning network for kids. HeartFirst Kids is an online community where children can practice using social media safely and kindly while learning essential life skills, such as emotional intelligence, empathy, mindfulness, and stress resilience. We would love to invite your children ages 7-12 to join us in a class.

"Life *is* school!"

~ Arianna Fox

CHAPTER THREE

A New Paradigm of Youth

By Arianna Fox, Age 15

"Success is no accident. It is hard work, perseverance, learning, studying, sacrifice, and most of all, love of what you are doing."

- Pelé, Brazilian Soccer Player

All the best stories start with *"Once upon a time,"* don't they?

So, climb upon a comfy couch and get ready for the story of a young girl who had always thought she had to wait until she was older to achieve her dreams. This story contains twists and turns, good and bad scenarios, and successes and failures.

This is the story of a continuing trek to success—and *a new paradigm of youth.*

Once upon a time, a young girl (AKA me) was moving around near the fireplace, keeping her—er, my—constantly hyper self very active with a few dances as my parents sat on the nearby couch. Then, I stopped: A massive revelation hit me, and I *immediately* had to tell my parents.

I went up to them and said with a look of dead seriousness and a tone of voice equivalent to that of Minnie Mouse, "I want to be an *author* when I grow up."

My parents immediately supported my decision and were excited to hear that I was so determined, but they asked one important question before further discussion: **"*Why wait?* Why not start now? Why wait until you're an adult to achieve your success?"**

And, at four years old, my tiny little mind was blown.

> *"Don't wait for the right opportunity. Create it."*

> ### - George Bernard Shaw, Playwright, Critic and Polemicist

Now, at fifteen, I am a girl entrepreneur, triple and best-selling author, motivational speaker, actress, voiceover talent, and teen influencer—but back then, I thought all those things were aspirations of what I could do when I'd become an adult, not things I could work on *right then*.

You see, I had always heard the question, "What do you want to be when you grow up?" and never once thought that I could do what I wanted to do in life at a young age.

So, dear reader, I shall take you to one more scene in this story of mine: that of the commencement of my motivational speaking business.

I was sound asleep in my bedroom. It was late 2016, and I was around ten years old. I was resting on the pillow as the fan gently blew behind me. Then, the door slowly creaked open, revealing the faces of my daddy and mommy.

They entered with smiles as they cooed, "Good morning." After I woke up, we began chatting as I started my daily morning routine.

As we were casually conversing, my daddy's eyes widened, a new idea surging through his mind as he asked, "What if you became a motivational speaker, and you spoke to kids about how to succeed, and you influence them to achieve their dreams while they're young?"

My immediate answer was, "*YES.*"

Apart from writing, my other main passion was to inspire people, but when I was younger, I never knew quite how to do it. So, when my parents suggested the idea of becoming an inspirational speaker, I couldn't help but agree with an ecstatic grin.

Now, these things—writing, owning a business (AKA entrepreneurship), and inspiring others at a young age are all part of a new paradigm of youth. In the old days, it was rare to see a young child with impressive entrepreneurial achievements. Sure, there were always child prodigies, but the trend of children, teens, and youth doing great things at an early age was not nearly at the point it is now. Whether you are a young person, a parent of one, an educator of one, or simply an adult who wishes to help, know that there is a rise in young entrepreneurship and talent—a shift from the old paradigm to the new.

A large part of that aforementioned "new paradigm" is that of education when it comes to us, the youth; in fact, the very title of this book is *A New Paradigm of Education*. And education—especially learning—just so happens to be one of my favorite subjects.

I am and have been homeschooled my whole life. I love this experience so much and always have; there is something about the creativity one can use to write an essay, the curiosity that gets satisfied when one performs a science experiment, or even the excitement one feels when one can learn about their ancestors in history. These are the things about which I am the most passionate—the things that fuel my excitement for learning.

Many people ask me, "Arianna, how do you balance life and school?" The answer to that question is fairly simple: **Life *is* school!**

Throughout the entirety of my life, my parents have helped support my creativity and foster a learning environment. So, wherever I go, whether I stay home and learn on a computer or travel with my parents to a chamber mixer for our family business, I'm always learning. To add to that, I'm always trying to understand the most important things to me and my life. I am a writer and a lass who deeply loves words and languages, so subjects like English and Spanish greatly interest me and will aid me in the future. However, you might be an artist or a musician—then you might find art or music to be the most fascinating school subjects. That is the beauty of tailored education (even if your school systems aren't so tailored and must develop a love for learning on your own.) You can pick what interests you and what you think will help you in the future.

As I mentioned, my parents always fostered a love of learning, even when it was difficult for me to concentrate on my schoolwork as a child. This is part of what began my entrepreneurial journey. I've always been a somewhat hyperactive girl, and my parents found it increasingly hard to get me to focus on sitting still and reading or watching a video, as I constantly needed to move around. So my parents came up with an idea for "Extreme Time," which is essentially a full hour for me to go as ballistic as I wished—to get all my energy out by dancing, pretending, and such. It instantly increased my concentration level when I sat down for schoolwork. This is just one of the many ways my parents used quick-witted problem-solving to help make education more fun.

Speaking of *fun*, to me, fun is one of the key components of fully learning any given subject. Studies have shown that people remember facts, learn languages, and even memorize words when they enjoy themselves and find it interesting; put simply, **you learn better when you have fun.**

One of the things I find quite fun is entrepreneurship. I previously mentioned going to chamber mixers and being an entrepreneur; I even shared the story of how I began my business and said that it is all part of the new paradigm. That is something I've been noticing for quite some time now. Back then, it was much rarer to see a child owning a business, save the old-fashioned lemonade stands you may have heard of a few times. Nowadays, young entrepreneurs—from young kids still in elementary school to teenagers about to hit adulthood—are much more common, and soon, I almost wonder if entrepreneurship in youth will be even more popular than entrepreneurship in adults.

Either way, youth business-owning is one of my favorite aspects of the new paradigm because this means that children have entrepreneurial communities to support them. They're encouraged not only to take action (e.g., starting a candle company) but also *produce* action (e.g., selling candles and creating revenue off of them)—and even make money from it if possible.

The truth is, whether you are a young person who wants to be an entrepreneur, an author, an artist, a musician, or practically *any* career path you wish to choose, it is all up to you when you decide to take action. When people ask me how I find motivation, I tell them I don't search for it; I *create* it. So, whatever your passion is—whatever it is that you love, that you enjoy doing, even if it feels more like work than fun sometimes—don't wait for adulthood or inspiration, but pursue it with all your heart, and above all, *never give up.*

You Rock, Dream Big, and You Got This!

"There is no better school or learning experience for any soul than to come to Earth."

~ Julie Ferris and Karen Goodson

CHAPTER FOUR

The Portal of Potential

By Karen Goodson and Julie Ferris

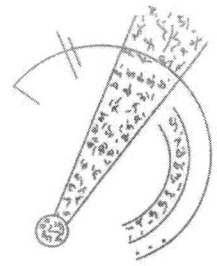

Authors' Introduction

The Portal of Potential is a co-creation between Karen, Julie, and the Council of Light for the Portal.

The Portal of Potential is a bridge with a vibrational frequency that can help you move from the world of duality to what many call New Earth. It grows continually and creates over eight places and spaces where you can find your hidden tools, skills, and abilities and where you can cleanse and regenerate your energy, connect with your soul family, and so much more.

The following story shows you how, once you enter the portal, you are drawn by your soul to visit whichever place is right for you at the time. It may look as if our avatars are bouncing from one place to another without any sense of purpose or direction, that is, if we look at it from the world of duality, where things have to be right or wrong, good or bad.

We invite you to follow these adventures from the view that everything *is* because it exists outside of time as we know it.

On the next page, you will find some of the places our three avatars visit in this story.

Places in The Portal of Potential

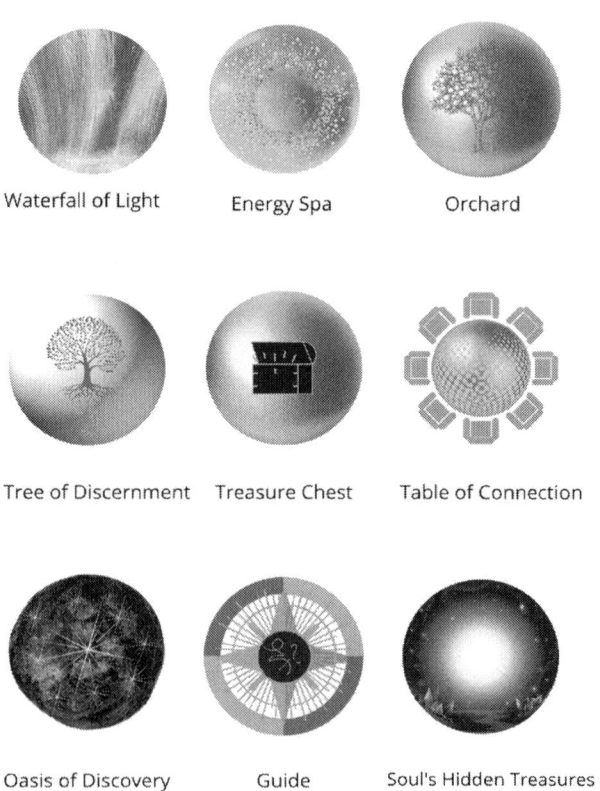

Waterfall of Light   Energy Spa   Orchard

Tree of Discernment   Treasure Chest   Table of Connection

Oasis of Discovery   Guide   Soul's Hidden Treasures

As you follow the adventures of these beautiful souls, you may feel like drawing, making notes, or expressing yourself through movement or another creative medium to help bring this into your conscious awareness and ground it into your reality.

The Golden Portal of Potential

This chapter will take you on a journey to show what the experience of the soul can be as it awakens to its true purpose on Earth at this moment. Your soul has chosen to incarnate now, and we will show you how to access the beauty within your soul. There is so much energy within your soul imprint that it cannot break through. You have created the systems you live within in many ways. They block the true you, who is longing to break through and connect with your soul tribe. Are you keen to know how to communicate with your soul tribe?

If you are in the physical form of a child, then you are often subject to the limitations of the education systems wherever you reside on the planet. These systems are very limiting and do not allow the soul to grow, learn, or experience what it wishes to feel. The old paradigm curriculums that exist right now are designed to stifle the soul's development.

So, let us break free from the old confines and discuss new ways of being. The ultimate aim of our work, through the *Portal of Potential,* is to allow all you beautiful souls to connect with *your* purpose for being here and with your soul tribe.

As you connect with your soul tribe, you learn new skills. You connect with the innate abilities you had to forget to incarnate in this lifetime.

The *Portal of Potential* is designed to bring families together. So, very often, beautiful star children are born into families at different stages of awakening. Family members may have some idea that the world is changing around them and that it can be lighter and better, but some may become stuck within the confines of the systems.

The portal is designed to help you, the parent, connect with *your* spiritual self and soul tribe, allowing the star child that may be within you to feel safe to express itself. This provides a safe space for your child to be the fully aware star child they truly are.

So, you could look at this portal as being created to help the parent open up to their spirituality and to help the child learn how to cope with the human experience because the human experience can be at complete odds with the spiritual or the world of light from which we all come.

We now bring you a divinely orchestrated story of three beautiful souls as they travel toward unity. They are the Mother, the Young One, and the Elder.

They travel toward unity because that is where we are going on this Earth as we follow the path of awakening. But you are here to learn about our views on education, how education can and will change in ways, in the days and in the times to come.

We see many different ways of connecting with the souls of those who are here to learn. You may have understood by now that we feel everybody needs to learn. Everybody is a teacher, a mentor, a coach, or a student, irrespective of age, ability, or any other factor.

We are all one; therefore, each individual has something to contribute to the growth and development of our fellow soul tribe members.

As we grow as human beings, we learn to connect more with our souls and, therefore, with all there is. This means we associate with all realms: the animals, the elementals that we cannot see, the fairies, the elves, the pixies, and the dolphins within the ether rather than the sea. Therefore, there are many different realms for you to connect with and many other things to learn.

We ask you to open your minds as you allow yourselves to learn and share your existing skills and knowledge of living as a human being, an awakened star on Earth, living in partnership with the Earth, not enslaved to systems such as the banking or school systems. So many of you are already aligned with these ancient realms and sharing your connection through play, imagination, and magic.

The Portal is about full sovereignty, learning to be your full sovereign self, and discovering what you came here to be as you access your true soul mission.

So, we share with you the adventures of three Avatars, the Mother, the Young One, and the Elder, to show you how this process can work. As you follow their adventures, you may feel as if you are there with them, sharing the experience of the *Portal of Potential*.

The *Portal of Potential* is a process and a multi-dimensional space that enables all souls who enter to learn things to have beautiful experiences and joyous adventures. Every step of the journey holds you safely as you develop the ability to connect with the rest of your soul tribe and yourself.

How important is it for us to connect with ourselves? Well, we tend to forget! We have all chosen to incarnate here partly because we wish to help Gaia, Mother Earth, change her experience and raise her vibration. We also decided to have this adventure for our soul advancement.

When we choose to have this adventure, there is no better school or learning experience for any soul than to come to Earth. Furthermore, there are very few other places within the galaxy where the soul can experience duality. Therefore, it is a much sought-after experience.

Of course, when you are in human form, feeling in the depths of despair, perhaps it is hard to imagine this, but we assure you that your mission is one that you chose and is something your soul and many other souls have been longing to experience for millennia.

Enjoy following the three Avatars as they journey through the *Portal of Potential* to New Earth with Julie and Karen.

The Portal of Potential to New Earth

They rest momentarily at the entry pillars. Ahead, the soul pathway explodes into flurries of pathways that move and meander through the landscape. Pools of water shimmer in the hazy heat, and the air carries the freshness of the water to those who are thirsty. Ancient trees intersect the landscape, and lushness is everywhere for those who look.

None of the three sees the other at the entrance. They are there with their thoughts. Each Avatar will choose their own path.

The energy begins to hum as a scroll falls into each of their hands. Then, finally, it is time for them to make their *choice*.

Of whether to enter.

A faint flash of golden light causes the Mother and the Elder to look up from their scrolls. Wrinkling their brows, they soon return to reading, slowly, carefully.

Young One: I'm in! I'm entering a tube that is not a tube. It is a sphere, yet tubular. The tubes surround the sphere. They are the sphere, yet they are within the sphere.

Guide: The Young One has entered! I knew this beautiful soul would enter first with such openness, joy, and willingness to explore. There is no welcome pack needed for this one! They have stepped on to the place of clarity, where you are open and honest with yourself. There is nobody else you need to influence or be influenced by.

Welcome to the journey, Young One! You will meet your soul family if you are not already with them. There is always a choice of where to go.

I smile as they gaze in open-mouthed wonder at the landscape, the cascading rainbow streams from the Waterfall of Light, the fierce golden glow emitting from an open treasure chest, trees laden with fruit, settled around an oasis pool of silver sparkles…

Young One: Do I go for the Waterfall of Light, or do I need to collect my tools from the Treasure Chest of Light?

Guide: Ask your soul to make a choice. If you choose to shower in the Waterfall of Light, you are cleared of any dense energies you may have brought with you through this Golden Portal of Potential.

In an expression of pure joy, the Young One weaves through the waterfall's cascades. Rainbow light refracts into the atmosphere as their beautiful soul expresses its true essence.

Young One: Where shall I go next? I see so many exciting things here. Look at the oasis. Shall I go to the Oasis of Discovery?

Look at the beautiful Temple of Light! So much choice. I want to try them all, but something is calling me back to the girl with the Ten Cloaks. There is a nice comfortable chair, and I immerse myself in the adventures of the girl with the Ten Cloaks. I see it as if it is on a multi-dimensional screen, and it is as if I feel her adventures. I experience them all as if I am the girl with the Ten Cloaks.

Guide: As the Young One sits and reads, their world is that mountain. It is as if they become the girl with the Ten Cloaks, embarking on the mysterious quest to which her soul has called her.

At the entrance, the Mother finishes reading. Her brain, now overloaded with streams of analysis of the scroll's content, surrenders to her body, which steps through the pillars in an instant. I welcome this beautiful soul. The landscape fades into the background as, together, we look at the tree. Tall. Rooted. Ancient. Connected. And more. The Mother steps up to discover.

Mother: I'm sitting underneath the tree, this Tree of Discernment. This place gives me stability. When I touch the tree, I feel it breathe, giving me breath, space, and strength.

There are many paths that I could take. So many places and routes, but I must sit here for a while to connect with myself.

I find I need to create a new me, one that breaks free from my parents, their parents, and their way of doing things. The way of doing things within our family has been the same for generations, and it is not so easy to let go. It is not so easy to create the true me.

So, I find the Tree of Discernment is my friend. I listen as I sit, and I am listening to myself. As I look up and listen, some leaves fall gently from this tree, and I gather them. They are like pearls of wisdom for me. They are my pearls of knowledge, but I am not ready to read them all. It is still so overwhelming, so I place them in my treasure chest.

I read one, and it had a symbol. This symbol asks me to call an animal friend to help me start this journey, my journey within.

Maybe I wish to choose a bird to help me fly or a strong animal for strength and courage, but I prefer a butterfly, for that is what speaks to me now. But I know this may change along the pathways, so I keep this leaf close to me, so I can be reminded that I don't have to walk alone.

Guide: The Mother calls. A glorious butterfly materializes to accompany her, to replace the weariness of the spirit that has been with her for so long. Her stride lengthens as she spies a delicious pool of water ahead, cocooned in youthful foliage, calm, restful, an Energy Spa to release, relax, and rejuvenate on a profound level.

Mother: I am going into the Energy Spa, actually into the water. I'm sitting in the hot bubbly water, like a space bubble around me. No one is demanding anything of me at this moment. This is my time to find myself, so I go into my bubble to rest.

Guide: Journeying into her bubble, the Mother is going to meet her soul.

At the entrance, wishing to reacquaint with his soul and purpose, the Elder enters with the resolve of one seeking to remember. The remembering has started.

Elder: I am within a family. I have taken the appearance of an elderly person, as this is non-threatening, but I am a higher being, coming to remember. I remember what I may have forgotten, but I cannot remember if I have forgotten it.

First, I need this sludgy stuff washed off, peeled off because I am embedded in the Earth, but my spirit wishes to fly and to remember. So, I am along the pathway, and I need to dunk myself quickly to get rid of this sludge. By the Energy Spa, there is a dunking pool. So, I am dunking myself in white light.

That feels much better. I feel lighter and can fly around now, and I am looking from above at all the places in the pathway that could help me remember what I am here for and how to do it. I am sure I know how to do it, or I wouldn't have come, but then I have things to learn. Guide: Welcome beautiful soul and galactic friend. You've let go of the weight of those old bones at last! I honor your soul of deep wisdom.

The golden light of the landscape buzzes as the Elder flexes the freedom of his soul.

Elder: I am walking on grids of light, like over a dome that encapsulates the pathway. Sliding down these golden lights around the shape is like riding a roller coaster. It is so much fun, and as I do it, those last bits of that lower density stuff have to go. They have to go.

As I slide along this roller coaster, the light is so bright and powerful that all that bad stuff goes, and immediately, I am next to the Young One.

We smile at each other, for we both know. We both know that, if we so wanted, we could sit around the Table of Connection for a while, connecting, but we both have our journeys, and I will start on my journey of remembering the Oasis of Discovery.

Guide: Rising from the comfortable chair, the Young One sparkles with illumination.

Young One: The last cloak has gone, and I realize I am that wise person. Oh yes.

Next is the Oasis of Discovery. Ah, there is a guide on the path. Guide, what happens if I go this way?

Guide: The choice is all yours. You can go into the Oasis of Discovery and have an adventure and find some tools that will help you tune into your soul purpose, your soul destiny, why you incarnated, and why you are here now. Or, you may feel you need to go to the Treasure Chest of Light. Many tools in the chest will help free you of any heavy burdens you carry and want to get rid of.

Young One: Yes, I want to rummage in the Treasure Chest of Light. Oh, look at that!

Guide: The Young One holds a majestic staff aloft. Carved light symbols twist their way around its length like a golden serpent. Alive. Powerful.

Young One: Ah, this is the staff of fire, yes, the staff of fire!

What do I do with it?

Guide: So, you hold it, and the guidance rushes through your light body, all levels and layers, and you will suddenly know how to use it and what to use it for.

And you aim this staff of light at a little spot on your body that feels a bit dense or heavy or maybe it is that backpack that belongs in another realm. So let's take it off. Oh yes, so much better.

Fire dances in the air and, from above, an ancient energy force swoops down. This pure, winged creature opens its heart, and a deep sound calls the Young One.

Young One: Oh, look, there is a dragon, my fire dragon! My fire dragon wants to take me for a ride. Look, where am I going now? I'm soaring through all realms as I explore this beautiful pathway leading me to New Earth.

I fly high above and look over. Am I ready for New Earth? No, not quite.

Ah, I can see my dragon is now taking me to an orchard. Yes, there is an orchard on the edge of the Oasis of Discovery. My dragon gently places me down, and I leave my staff of fire with him for safe keeping, and there is this beautiful red, shiny apple calling to me. I can see right through it. It contains a fantastic tool for me. It is light. It is a tool I can take. The girl's energy scanner is the one she told me about in the Ten Cloaks. I can accept that now, take it into my heart, into my third eye, so that I may see. I will be able to scan anything to determine its intentions toward me.

Guide: The Young One brings the gridded shape of light through their heart into their third eye.

Young One: Suddenly, everything looks different. I see more beauty in this wonderous pathway of red and green moss.

Guide: The Young One is connecting with their tools! The fire staff and the energy scanner have answered their dear friend's call, their fire dragon. I feel the expansion of the Young One, and there are so many more tools that this Young One has created. So many more!

Young One: What is that light coming out of the soles of my feet? I stepped onto an extraordinary place that opened the portals within my feet's soles, allowing the light to shine in and out. It feels like I am walking on air, but there is no gravity in this place or space.

I'm not ready to look into my soul yet.

I'm going to the Temple of Light for a rest in a healing pod.

Guide: With this intention, the Young One transports themselves to the Energy Spa to rest in their healing pod and integrate these energies.

Closeby, but unseen, the Young One's Mother is in her Bubble of Light in the Energy Spa. I feel how desperately she needs to connect with her soul. Without this connection, she will keep reaching out and missing that soul connection with the Young One. The Young One chooses to be with the Mother. They decided her soul, but if she is not with her soul, there can be no genuine soul connection between them.

Mother: In my Bubble of Light, the symbols move through me, and I write my own. I'm writing my own on my Bubble of Light. What I want is connection. I like the connection to myself, my true self. I want to find and live it, so, within this bubble, I am writing my symbols for connection—my soul symbol for connection to myself.

I write this symbol, and I have a mirror so I can look at it from all angles, and I can embody this symbol. I can step into this symbol. It is me to whom I wish to connect.

Maybe I have to go and face some challenges that I have not yet released, but this doesn't feel frightening. I have a light staff, the road is lit, and there is a Guide there to help my animal friend and me. It is like looking at a screen. I don't have to be in that situation again. I have to look at the screen and see the challenge presented to me and what I did, but I don't feel it. I am not in it. I am just observing the screen and choose to release it.

I have in front of me an enormous sheet of golden paper, and I can place that episode, that challenge. I can wrap it in this paper for I have learned, and it is released, and it goes. I can choose whether to see more episodes on this machine for viewing challenges. I can determine if there are more episodes for me to watch, if I want to, or if that is enough for now.

I feel that, maybe, I can watch one more. I watch it on that screen, observing, and I am ready to release this part too, so I wrap it in the golden paper, and it is gone.

I feel much lighter now as I walk along the path, and I feel like going to the Waterfall of Light for a quick shower.

Guide: She is getting to know her soul! The Mother is discovering the beauty of her soul frequency. My heart is full. I know she will move towards the Table of Connection to embody her soul imprint at this golden, circular table of light that transcends many layers and levels.

The Table of Connection is a beautiful consciousness, pure, evolving, and coded with deep love. It is there, stable but fluid, rippling a golden light that calls these dear souls. Each seat belongs to the essence of a soul within a soul family. Their symbol is imprinted into its memory, and it knows their soul song. It knows the harmonious song of this soul family. To sit in your soul is to connect with your soul and remember who you are and what you are here to do. To sing your soul song embodies who you are and calls out to your soul family with profound love and connection.

There are many routes to connecting with your soul, your higher self, and your soul mission. So, I smile as I see the Elder move gracefully in the oasis's clear waters.

Elder: I am bathing in the lake. I am paddling in the Oasis of Discovery. There are silver fish swimming around my feet. I wish to submerge in this water and, as I do, be immersed in the pool of remembering. So, I swim, and the fish become light as I swim through silver light. They guide me until I reach my table of light, a round table with golden scrolls, and I am writing. I am writing my agreed path, and I am with my soul. I look up at myself, and I smile, and we smile, for we both know who we are, but I need to touch the writing on the scroll of truth to find ' out again, to remember my path, my contract, and I do this. I place my hand on the writing, and those golden symbols flow through my body, and my body expands. I am light.

The other me, at the table, hands me a tool. It is mine. It is mine! It is a staff. It is my staff of wisdom, and in this staff is my wisdom gathered over millennia, over many lifetimes. So, I take my white team and need to re-enter the pool of remembering, so that I can start doing what I had to remember to do.

I come out of the pool, and I now remember! I could go straight through the gateway into the New Earth, but I am here to weave energy first. Some parts might need strengthening, so again, I go, and I look from above at the places that are fading, where the light is fading, and I go down and weave the energy to strengthen that light. And I see my family along the pathway, and I can help them find their way.

Guide: The Elder sees his dear Earth family on their pathways from an eagle's eye. The sun casts a golden light through the landscape, caressing the fresh leaves of ancient trees, dancing nimbly over the waters, and stretching its rays to fill the sky. The Mother is glowing from her Waterfall of Light as she walks towards the Table of Connection, her beautiful butterfly at her side. She follows her golden footprints imprinted in the pathway to remember the way. The Elder sees how the light from these footprints begins to dim as she clouds her eyes with self-doubt.

He sees the Young One glide along the red and green moss, uplifted by the powerful light flowing through his feet from and to the Earth. Then, the Young One enters the Energy Spa's profound sanctuary to rest and grow.

Young One: While I am resting, I'm in a beautiful, beautiful spa bath, and I'm pulling symbols into the water. Ooh, and some are dissolving in the water, and some are sticking on the outside—scrolls of light. I've decided to rest and lie

*here, feeling deeply relaxed. Now, I am ready to go back
to the Oasis of Discovery to feel into my soul journey, but
there is something I need to do first. Ah, the Meditation, the
Meditation of the Blue Headdress of Clarity.*

Guide: As the Young One settles in to listen, reclaim, and
activate crystal clarity, the Elder prepares to help his family.

*Elder: I have woven a light carpet, like a flying carpet,
which can be placed around the Energy Spa. Often, doubts
and uncertainty come. To sit on this carpet is to uplift one's
energy. To rise above one's sludge, and to fly. When you pass,
those places you may need to go may intensify in the light like
a giant spotlight. So, maybe a family member needs to go to
the orchard or the Oasis of Discovery. But oh, the Young One
has jumped on the carpet as well. It can be fun. It can be fun.*

Guide: How connected these two souls are on many levels
and layers. I can't wait for them to remember who they
are and what they are here to do. The Young One goes to
the Oasis of Discovery to find out! This will be a cosmic
revelation for the Young One.

*Young One: There is a guide again at the Oasis of Discovery.
Guide, can I ask your advice? Yes, it is always within, is
it not? A critical lesson of sovereignty is knowing we have
everything we need.*

*Ah, the Blue Headdress of Clarity is on my head, and I feel this
beautiful sparkly cloak being placed around my shoulders as I
face the waters of the Lake of Discovery, the Oasis of Discovery.*

*It is almost as if I am watching a film, but it is multi-faceted
and multi-dimensional.*

I am seeing myself in a spaceship—new origins. My origins as a star child, waiting for the humans to open the door. Yes, the Earth is smiling. I am connecting to my origins. Yes.

Guide: An electrifying pulse of belonging surges through the Young One as they remember their origin amongst the stars. Their beautiful soul mission starts to awaken in their memory as they are transported to witness a monumental moment on their spaceship—the moment when the bridge is connected to this life.

What a remembrance! My heart is so full of love. The Elder, too, is plugging into his soul mission!

Elder: I have remembered what I am here to do. I'm going to the Table of Connection, for inside the table, there is a Crystal of Community made of many crystals. This Crystal of Community must be activated so when all arrive at the table, the bonds of community, the energies, can start to flow through the family in preparation for the entrance to the other gateway, to the New Earth.

I am at the Table of Connection, and the Young One helps me, of course. We laugh because it is like screwing in a light bulb and pressing some things and something is activated. The Crystal of Community, made up of many crystals, is active.

Guide: A myriad of colors shoots into the sky. The Young One and Elder watch as the light weaves upwards, dancing, expressing the pure joy of each soul in this soul family for co-creating a new strand of life, a new way of being: connected, co-created, collaborative. The here and beyond witness in celebration the activation of this soul family.

Knowing that there is no space for self-doubt in the light, the Mother chooses to open her heart to receive more. She arrives at the Table of Connection.

Mother: I wish to connect more deeply in my seat at the table. So, I sit at my part of the table with my soul imprint and feel comfortable and at home. Something comes out of the middle of the table, but I am not ready to look into that yet.

I am not yet ready to see who else is around the table. I need to discover more about my pathway and what I can do on my pathway, so I go to the Oasis of Discovery.

I ask the guide for help, and he points me to another tree, a sapling. I know this is me, the true me, and I need to nurture myself. A watering can is in the corner, golden with symbols that dance, and I need to choose what to put in my watering can. First, I prefer water and fire, for this tree needs energy, and my pathway needs energy. Second, I know that, later, my tree will need air and Earth.

There is a light source here, like a tap of light, and I know that being a parent is essential. So, I fill the can with these beautiful waves of light because I wish to be filled with this light.

This light connects to my child, and it is like we are swimming in a pool of rainbow light together, ducking and diving and swimming and laughing, and this is a magic pool that regenerates our relationship. Where sometimes there is friction and frustration, this helps lubricate the wheels that turn in our relationship so that they flow and are one, and we connect with the heart, and so, I wish to stay in this pool for a while.

I know I am also here to help guide my child, which means guidance in the way of being human and some battles. Battles of will. So, I wish to seek a tool to help me, and I remember the leaves given to me by the Tree of Discernment. So, I pull out another leaf, and it calls in a tool to help me so these battles are not too big and not too fierce and are the right ones.

Guide: With each experience in the landscape, this dear soul is connecting more with her sovereignty and her wonderful mission as a soul and as a Mother. As she sheds even more layers, making space for more light, her vibration soars, and her light connects with her child. She is tuning into the higher realm elements of water and fire, which will bring her flow and energy along her journey. This beautiful soul is elevating her pathway.

Now the Young One asks to connect with the elements, with the Earth to ground their path!

Young One: I'm now drawn to connect more with Mother Earth. Guide, can you show me how to connect with Mother Earth?

Guide: I hand the Young One ancient scrolls of light.

Young One: I feel myself holding the scrolls of the elements, holding them and standing upon them, absorbing the energy through the light portals in my feet and holding them up to my blue headdress eye, holding them to my heart and feeling them connecting with my soul.

There are other dragons now. For example, a Dragon of Air and a Dragon of Light are taking me to the Treasure Chest of Light because there are more tools for me.

I cannot see which tool is for me. Which device should I choose, Guide?

Guide: Before I can breathe, the Young One has already chosen, and what an aligned choice!

Young One: It is like I am unwrapping a parcel, and within the parcel is a sword. Ah, is this my sword? My sword of light. Ah, this will help me cut through any obstacles I face or challenges as I find my true destiny.

I feel I am ready to go through the gateway. Am I ready? I sense I am not to go through alone. I think I must wait for my soul family. Everyone in my family is at a different stage, in other places, on the pathway.

I am going back to the Temple of Light. I feel I would like another shower in the Waterfall of Light and then go back to the Oasis of Discovery. Although I want the Oasis of Discovery, there is something different for me. Ooh, this is funny! Under the tree, I find the disc of light, and as I throw it, it spins around and lights up every little dark space so I can see even more clearly.

Guide: Within her journey of light, the Mother is now ready to meet the Treasure Chest of Light and reclaim a sacred tool.

Mother: I am taken immediately, as if I can fly up in the air, to the Treasure Chest of Light. I open it, and inside is a heart, a pink heart, and it glimmers and glistens. I see two doors inside, and I open the doors, and inside is a tiny nugget of gold. So I am called to place this in my heart and to follow my heart.

This nugget helps to illuminate my wisdom more clearly. My wisdom as a mother or father, as a loved one, so that I know that, when we have to battle, it is for the right reason and not just to put forward my way or the way of my parents and grandparents. It is discernment.

85

I am tapping into my soul imprint. When I feel this is fading, the guide tells me to stand on the Foot Portal of Light and to intend for my soul imprint to be illuminated so that I do not fall back into my old ways and the ways of the past generations of my family.

Guide: They are close to connecting at the Table of Connection! Their hearts are open, and they have uncovered much of who they are and what they are here to do as individuals and within a soul family. I witness in celebration as these custodians take their places at their table.

The Elder, a holder of light and weaver of energy, is a beloved member of this soul family.

Elder: The table is ready for those in the family who wish to connect, so I may sit here for a while because I am bathed in crystal light, like a beacon, a torch. The Young One is here too, but we decide there is still more to do, help, journey, and experience within this place.

So, we fly and slide down the lights and try to assist the family by weaving the energy. We incorporate the energies of the crystal throughout so that, when they are connected to the pathway through their feet, they may receive these energies.

Guide: The Mother, holder of deep love, a guide to the human realm, and beloved member of this soul family.

Mother: I have gone right now to the Table of Connection! Ah, next to me, ooh, how my heart fills with joy. Next to me is my child, talking, talking to me about what has happened to them, telling stories. Then, after a short break, we hold hands and then off again. There is more exploring to do, and I feel like my child is looking for the rest of us from around the table.

We have connected, and when the next one is ready to join, I am sure we will be taken back to the Table of Connection, so we can connect more deeply.

But for now, I will go back to the Energy Spa and regenerate and look at the leaves I have helping me, stage by stage.

Guide: The Young One, star child, holder of deep love, weaver of energy and light, a beloved member of this soul family.

Young One: I can see more members of my family. They are kind of appearing as if they have been in the mist. We gather at the round table, like King Arthur's table. It is the Table of Connection.

We are sharing our experiences and talking about our missions. It feels incredible to realize how similar we are now. We didn't feel like this when we were in purely human form when we started on this journey.

Here we are now, working together, so that we can come up with a plan so that we can go through the gateway together.

Guide: These souls come together within their great wisdom and deep love to continue on their soul pathways, to embody their soul missions, not alone, but with each other to help and guide. For the guide is within, within themselves and each other. As they work together to plan a way to enter the gateway as a soul family, my final act is to place the ancient golden scroll once more on their table.

When the scroll lands and the energy hums, the Elder, the Mother, and the Young One look together. United. Connected. A family of beautiful souls who will change the world.

Authors' Conclusion

We hope you enjoyed following the journey of our three beautiful Avatar souls. The story takes you into the multi-dimensionality of potential in the world. The conscious mind may find it difficult to hold all of the threads together, but you can be sure your soul resonates with it one hundred percent.

The Portal of Potential is not just the subject of this story. We are co-creating a board game, workshops, and courses. Personal sessions are also available now.

As mission souls, we embed quantum technologies in everything we do here on Earth. Quantum tools and techniques connect directly with the soul, allowing the human mind to join when ready.

When you and your soul tribe reach the Table of Connection simultaneously, you are ready to co-create New Earth, new paradigms in education, community, and all aspects of life.

Resources:

The Choice is a short story that invites readers to review their life path and its alignment with their soul mission.

The Ten Cloaks is the story of a girl's perilous journey up a mountain, facing challenges and obstacles, shedding cloaks as she learns to believe in herself.

If you feel guided to read *The Choice* or *The Ten Cloaks* by Karen Goodson and Julie Ferris, please follow this link to access these stories as a gift https://bit.ly/3LbbsFc

"I see my connection to nature and how it's essential that our education system also teaches our students about this connection. Teaching *for* sustainability, not just about it."

~ Ida Rahayu

CHAPTER FIVE

Connecting to Nature through Food in Education

By Ida Rahayu

I have been an educator since 2004, and teaching is one of my passions. I feel grateful to have had the opportunity to work at Green School Bali since 2012. It's been life-changing. The school and the community have opened my eyes to how I see my connection to nature and how it's essential that our education system teaches our students about this connection. This is something that not a lot of schools are focusing on. Teaching *for* sustainability, not just about it, especially in the public schools here in Indonesia. The type of holistic, wall-less, authentic, and student-centered education wasn't something I had when I was in school.

As a Javanese person, I am thankful that the island of Bali has welcomed me with a lot of love and beautiful energy. I feel at home. When I started working at the Green School Bali as an Indonesian language teacher, I had little to offer my students besides teaching my mother tongue. Two years later, the school decided to add a program called "Jalan-

Jalan," an Indonesian word that literally means taking a walk or traveling. The idea of this program is for students to be out and about, exploring, having real experiences, and connecting with communities. It's a mixed-age elective program, where students in grades six, seven, and eight can choose what they desire based on their passions.

Green School focuses on student-centered learning and getting students to choose what they are passionate about. As a teacher, I was to provide classes that gave students opportunities for experiential learning, based on their passions and strengths. At that time, I decided to give opportunities for students to have fun with cooking. I believe cooking is an important life skill they will need for the rest of their lives.

The cooking classes went well. The students had a lot of fun cooking anything they liked and eating together afterward. They made tacos, oatmeal cookies, chia pudding, ceviche, and much more. They found some recipes online and gathered some ingredients before class. However, I thought something was missing. I was wondering what the students were actually learning from the class. Apart from the cooking experience, something more meaningful and impactful had to be happening. So, I started learning more about food and nutrition. I would often invite teachers, who were chefs or nutritionists, to talk to the class. We had a parent, who is a nutritionist and owns one of the healthy food stalls at school, come in and share her expertise with the students. She shared information about nutrition, a healthy balanced diet, and the science behind tastes and how to combine them to create tasty meals. She also shared some healthy recipes. During these sessions, I learned alongside my students.

In 2016, I was granted a university scholarship for a year-long graduate certificate program in Permaculture Design. It was life-changing! I felt positive impacts both personally and professionally. From the course, I learned so much about sustainable living and better understood who I am as a part of the natural world. I believed that before I could teach it to others, I needed to do it myself. Understanding permaculture changed my perspective about loving nature.

At university, I joined the Nature Lover Club. We did a lot of hiking, rock climbing, white-water rafting, etc. I thought loving nature meant spending more time in nature, planting trees, and cleaning up the rivers or the oceans. Now, I understand it's beyond that. I think it's about understanding my role as *part* of nature. I am beautifully interconnected with all other living and nonliving things - plants, animals, microorganisms, fungi, water, air, soil, and many other things. Everything I do will impact those living things, and I should try my best to make a positive impact. One example is eating, an act which every living being needs to do to live. If I eat food that is grown organically in a way that regenerates the soil and ecosystem, I am making a positive impact. However, suppose I eat chemically fertilized and sprayed produce. In that case, I am making a negative impact by supporting the practice of farmers who deplete the soil and create an imbalance in the ecosystem. As part of the collective called nature, we must ensure that everything is balanced to survive. For me, loving nature means loving being a part of it and living in harmony with it. This is what I want to share with my students.

Using permaculture ethics and principles, I developed my cooking class into a more holistic project-based learning program, called Seeds to Table. The idea is to bring awareness to students about the impact of the food they eat on their health, the environment, and the society around them.

Looking at how we eat, generally, we are disconnected from our food. Our food system doesn't allow us to know where our food comes from, who grows the plants, how they're grown, who raises the animals, or how they are looked after. Even worse, sometimes we don't know what we put in our bodies. Our ancestors used to hunt and gather for food, getting all the nutrients they needed as it came from healthy, rich undisturbed soil. When humans started domesticating and cultivating plants and animals twelve thousand years ago, people searched less for food. These days, food is being marketed in highly processed forms, grown or raised with a high content of chemicals that pollute our bodies and our environment. I believe a new education paradigm enables us to connect back to the roots of food and nature and be truly **one** with it.

The cost to our health, the environment, and the resources used to produce a lot of convenient, fast foods is heartbreaking. The soil is depleted with chemicals used in fertilizers, the forests are being cut down for more agricultural purposes, and the biodiversity of animals has gone down due to deforestation and chemical sprays. These chemicals pollute the water, air, and soil, to name a few. Knowing all these facts made me realize how important it is for me as an educator to inspire my students to be more connected with the food they eat and inspire them to create a positive impact. Seeds to Table was designed for students not only to learn how to cook, but also to understand what makes a healthy and nutritious meal, as well as grow edible gardens from seeds and composting.

Students learn the whole cycle of food and are encouraged to connect with their food and the natural world.

What does the Seeds to Table program look like? It's a course where students learn how to grow seeds, plant seedlings into a garden bed, harvest their crops, cook using the ingredients they have grown, and compost any waste. The focus of the class is to use only local and seasonal ingredients, organic when possible, and generating zero waste. The students love cooking classes. It's mind-blowing what they create. For the cooking classes, I would normally share simple cooking techniques in the kitchen using simple ingredients they can use later. I like to allow them to cook whatever they want as long as it's healthy and sustainable. Valuing students' diverse creativity is the key to education, like valuing the diversity in nature helps it to thrive. Giving freedom to students about what they cook gives them a chance to explore and learn naturally. It's okay to make mistakes or fail, as there are a lot of lessons in the process. All I do in the kitchen during these cooking classes is make myself available if they need help, or sometimes I create something as well. I am always learning together with them.

I realized that running the Seeds to Table program for only one term was not enough time for my students to experience the whole process of planting and harvesting. They also did not have the opportunity to gain a deeper understanding of each element, like the plants or the soil, and to understand how the whole system works. Everything related to food is very complex. There are so many elements that should be explained deeper within this course. For example, when producing food in regenerative farming, we would focus more on perennial plants, and some plants would take at least six months to bear results.

In 2021, I had the opportunity to redesign and teach
Green Studies, a subject at Green School that focuses
on environmental science and stewardship. I used this
opportunity to develop Seeds to Table as a three-year course
for Middle School students to learn from grades six to eight. I
created a different focus for each grade. Grade six is focused
on soil, seeds, and medicinal plants. Grade seven focuses on
animals and how microorganisms are part of the ecosystem as
a source of our food. This includes composting. Grade eight
covers processing the harvest, ingredients, and enterprise
projects around food. The course is adaptable for all ages and
can be taught holistically rather than as a subject.

Seeds and Nursery

The grade six students would start with an introduction to
permaculture ethics, which consists of Earth Care, People
Care, and Fair Share. They learn about seeds and understand
the difference between hybrid and heirloom seeds and the
importance of planting heirloom seeds. Like anything else,
seeds are also becoming a commodity that companies are
monopolizing. A lot of seeds are being industrialized, and this
impacts our natural ecosystem.

Whenever I have the students grow something from seeds,
they can choose any seeds available for them to plant.
"What would you like to grow? Just think about what
you would like to cook later," I would often say to them.
It's satisfying to see how excited they are watching the
seeds they planted growing, which also gets me excited. I
remember one day a student came into class in the morning.
She rushed to the back balcony where we had our nursery

and shouted with excitement, "OMG, my rosella is growing. This is so cool!" She would come and check every morning and remember to water it. I know that feeling of awe and satisfaction to see the beauty of nature. Some students even gave their plants names, like Timothy for their tomato plants or Brittany for their butterfly pea. This particular student wrote in her reflection about her garden bed, saying, "It's challenging to see Brittany Butterfly Pea strangling Timothy Tomato." I loved how they used alliteration with a twist of humor to explore what happened with the plants they were growing.

Soil

Soil is the key to our food. To connect with our food means to communicate with the soil. Many of us do not understand the importance of healthy soil to maintain our existence on this planet. Healthy soil gives us the nutritious food we need to live and keeps our ecosystem in balance. Healthy soil is one of the solutions to climate change. However, more than a third of natural habitats, like forests, grassland, etc., have been cleared for agricultural purposes. Chemical fertilizer is increasingly used to grow our food, which depletes the soil, killing all the life inside it that is substantial. Depleted soil doesn't give us enough nutrients we need in our food. That's why it's important to connect more with the source of our food and what kind of soil it's been growing in.

Soil is a very complex topic, and so many elements around it need to be discussed. I would start by getting the students to understand the differences between healthy and unhealthy soil, what makes soil healthy and what causes soil to become unhealthy, the importance of healthy soil and what we can do to keep our soil healthy. The science of soil is my favorite subtopic—life under the dirt with all the microbes, insects, fungi, and mycelium network. Students also learn about the importance of mulch or ground cover to protect the earth.

Permaculture guild

This is another favorite subtopic; one way to keep the soil healthy is by planting a biodiversity of mostly perennial plants. Students learn which plants are local in Bali and which are not and how each plant, including weeds, has its function in the system. Students learn about how the natural ecosystem works and that we should use the pattern in nature as a guideline to design our garden. Each student would work in a group, sketch a garden, and make a list of what they want to grow. Seeing how excited they are to decide what to plant and collaborate is so encouraging. Although sometimes they don't agree with each other, this is when they learn how to respect the opinion of others, express their own ideas, and work as a team.

Planting, Maintenance, Harvesting

This is the fun part when the students get to plant the seedlings they have prepared. It's so beautiful how they all work together as a team, dividing jobs, composting from our compost stations, weeding, or collecting some dry Alang-Alang (Cogon grass we usually use for roofing) for mulch. Sometimes, we have damaged or worn-out Alang-Alang roofs, so we use that for mulching our garden. Every time we had a class, the first thing they wanted to do was go to their garden and check on their plants. Sometimes, we would sit together as a class and quickly reflect on how things were going, sharing what was going well in the garden and what issues might arise. If there are issues, we discuss why they happened and what the solutions might be. After a few months, I got the students to harvest whatever was ready and for them to cook in the kitchen. They loved it. When we did a quick circle before eating, the students would share. One student said, "It feels so good to eat something we plant ourselves. This way, I appreciate food even more, and it's good to know where this food comes from. I know it's good for my body, and I don't harm the environment."

Animals (chicken, bees and composting)

Growing our food regeneratively isn't possible without involving animals and other organisms. Students in grade seven look in-depth at the roles of animals in the ecosystem and how to take care of them. We focus only on certain animals, like chickens, insects (bees), and those who help with composting, like worms and black soldier flies. Although we have other animals like cows and pigs on campus, I don't focus on these animals. We do use cow manure to make our compost, though. For the chicken project last year, the students reorganized the chicken coop by designing a new house and fundraised to buy some of the materials and chickens. They built a new bamboo house for the chickens, prepared the deep litter system, and learned how to feed them properly. They also learned about black soldier flies, which help compost our food scraps and use the larvae as a nutritious food source for the chickens.

Food Health and Food Enterprise Project

At this stage, students explore the many elements of food that many people are unaware of. Students go deeper into the definition of food and food philosophy. For example, what is food to us? Why do we need food? What's the history of food as medicine; how does food impact our health and environment; what, where, when, and how do we eat? Yes, it's vital that we enjoy the food we eat, but it is also imperative to be *conscious* of our relationship with it. The students explored this topic individually, so they could express their opinions and ideas on the subject. They created a Google site with the purpose of finding a more profound connection with food and sharing their work with a bigger community to inspire them. At the end of this course, I asked for students' feedback, and they suggested that they should be able to use different platforms, not just websites. Next time, I would love to let the students use any media they are most interested in, such as creating a short documentary, podcasts, posters, artwork, etc. This is a way to connect with the students by listening to them and accommodating them when possible.

Once the students understand more about food, it's time for them to create something using natural ingredients. The idea of cooking classes is fun. They love it, and sometimes some students do not want to go to break as they enjoy cooking so much. But is cooking the only way? Of course not. It's nice sometimes to cook together and enjoy the meals as a community, but it is also lovely to add something a bit more interesting to the cooking activity. So, I invited the students to do a cook-off in a lesson we called Green MasterChef.

Green MasterChef challenges them to cook healthy and sustainable dishes. It's not only about cooking; there are a lot of skills and values that students can learn here. Collaboration is a big part of organizational skills, responsibility, creativity, trust, and sustainability. Students could plan what they want to make with the group and ensure they only use natural, fresh, local, and seasonal ingredients. Since we don't have every ingredient in our garden, I encourage students to connect with the food source. We visited farmers, connected with the suppliers, and found out where the ingredients come from, knowing that the production of it is not harming the environment. While planning, they would ask if certain ingredients were local. It sparked their curiosity. For example, a student asked, "Why don't olives grow here in Bali?" Another student replied, "Because this plant needs a certain climate to grow and produce fruit. Bali's climate isn't for it." They would name many ingredients they want to use and ask if they are local. If not, they would figure out how to use it in their dish. It's nice sometimes to be there listening to their conversation while planning their recipes. I am happy they have started being conscious of what they are cooking.

The Green Warung Enterprise Project

Another fun thing to add to the cooking classes is an enterprise project. It's a student-led project that they open and manage, the Green Warung. "Warung" is an Indonesian word for food stall or small restaurant. So, our warung is our school cafeteria.

I shared with my students the job openings, descriptions, and qualifications needed to fulfill each role. Each student went through the process from applying for the job they wanted to having a job interview. For the role of Head Chef, they needed to complete a cooking challenge. Students run the warung and, of course, they were paid their profit. Each student has a role based on what they are passionate about including management, accountants, cashiers, purchasing team, chefs, cooks, waiters, and marketing crew. I collaborated with the Green School finance department, marketing and communication team, and managers to help mentor the students so they could learn from real experts. Students learn from not only me but also our community.

It's beautiful to see the process and how they propose to get a loan from school to start the businesses and pay it back. When they start their project, not everything goes smoothly - they struggle with their communication skills and collaboration but manage to work on it; creating a healthy and sustainable menu is not easy. However, they still needed to make sure that other students liked it so they could sell it. Yes, students needed to ensure they sold healthy and sustainable food, but one day they decided to sell Rice Krispies. Of course, they had already made them, but I explained, "No, you are not selling them, and you know why. Unless you want to make a healthy version of Rice Krispies, then, yes." They understood and were not going to make them again. They did conduct an experiment to try to make a healthy version using red rice and dark chocolate, which was actually quite good.

Just like in a real business, the students each played a different role, and someone got fired as he wasn't doing his job properly. Some of the cooks came to me and said they weren't happy with the head chef as he wasn't helping his team, and it was hard to communicate with him. I suggested they speak with their general manager so they could make the decision to resolve the issue. After a long discussion with the team of students, the manager made the decision to let the head chef go and hired another one from the existing kitchen team. The old head chef then had to apply for another role that was available, like being a waiter or one of the marketing crew. It's amazing how consciously they handled this real-life scenario. One day, one of the teachers told me that he thought some students were hanging out in the classroom during break time. He tried to talk to them, and they said, "Excuse me, but we are having a very important meeting. We are about to fire someone." He exclaimed, "Wow, they are serious about their business!"

Another thing that happened like in real business, someone decided to resign. He thought the job was too hard for him to handle, so he decided not to continue. I told him that it was okay to step down, but he would need to write a resignation letter. After he resigned, I gave him the opportunity to choose any activity or a project he would like to do that was related to food, for example, gardening. This class really gave students the opportunity to learn a lot of life skills, to push themselves to try things they hadn't done before, to discover new strengths, and to recognize when they needed to take a step back. They learned how to deal with real-life successes and problems, both nice and challenging. For example, the students reflected that not everyone is nice in these kinds of on-the-job situations. The cashier said that some people were pleasant, but others were impatient, and it sometimes felt rude. The students learned resilience, compassion, and how to not take things personally, but instead to overcome all those challenges as a team.

During the pandemic, the school decided to minimize the crowd gathering, including in the Green Warung. So, we used the time for team-building activities and professional development. The kitchen team decided to experiment with making their pasta. We only had flour in our store cupboard, so they went to the chicken coop, collected some eggs, and stopped at the garden to pick some basil they had grown. Finally, the pesto pasta was ready. Last term, pasta was on their lunch menu, and it was very popular and always sold out.

Yes, this Green Warung project provided a lot of learning but also required a lot of evolution, not only for the students but also for me as a facilitator. All this gratitude encouraged me to give back to the island and community. Amazingly, Green School exists in Bali, but most students are not from Bali. They are from outside of Indonesia. No matter where they are from, students should have the opportunity to learn in this way. This is why I started sharing my knowledge with the local students. I was called to give back to the island and community by making Seeds to Table accessible to all local schools in Bali.

There is so much highly processed food sold in their canteens; almost all of them are packaged mostly in plastics. While several schools have good waste management, most schools in Bali do not. Some school waste would be picked up by a truck and put in landfills. I have seen it with my own eyes, and they burn the trash within the school compound. They do not understand the impact of this waste on their health and environment, so I created the Seeds to Table in Bali Schools program.

The idea of this program is a little different, as I am focusing more on waste management in local schools, with the objective that these schools start having proper waste management, an edible garden, a composting system, and cooking classes. As a starting goal, they are encouraged to use less plastic or to minimize as much packaging as possible. When I started this project, after school hours at Green School, I went to a few local schools to teach a group of students to grow food from seeds, make worm compost, sort out waste, and cook. It felt so rewarding to see how students appreciate having the opportunity to have an outdoor and hands-on class. They seemed to enjoy it. The principal of one of the schools told me how the kids checked on their garden every day and nibbled on tomatoes they grew in their garden.

After some time, I got busier and no longer had time to teach the program by myself. So, I decided to invite some of the teachers to a 4-day teacher training course so they could run the program at their schools without me. I encouraged these teachers to start being aware of the greater impact of growing, cooking, and eating food. Some great feedback I received was that teachers had begun growing their own food at home. One teacher told me how she went to a traditional market and brought all her containers and bags to reduce waste. She sent me a video that inspired her.

Another day, I went to a bulk store in Bali and ran into a teacher from another school. She told me that, because of me, she now goes to the shop more regularly and buys fresh produce instead of buying food with unnecessary plastic packaging and is also starting to cook healthier meals.

I believe our wisdom about caring for the planet comes from applying it ourselves - we can be role models to our students. One of my student's reflections after learning about medicinal plants shares this wisdom. "This class showed me how nature can help you and how nature gives better products than buying them at a store." Through food, we can bring up our future generations to connect more with their bodies and with nature.

Tips on how to start the *Seeds to Table* project in your school or home:

1. Start with yourself. Sit back and reflect on your diet and lifestyle. *What do you eat daily? Is it whole food, less processed, locally sourced, ecologically grown, or raised? Do you know where it comes from? How much waste do you create every day from your food? Do you separate them? Do you compost your organic waste? Do you recycle? If not, what happens to your daily waste? Is it ending up in a landfill site?*

2. Start growing food in your school or home. Even if you don't yet have a garden or land, it can be as simple as growing tomatoes or mint in a pot. Students can also design their pots or containers or reuse old jars.

3. Minimize going to supermarkets and buy less packaged stuff. You can connect with those who grow your food or raise the animals, if you eat animal products, by going to the closest farmer's market instead.

4. Growing food might not be accessible at the beginning. Also, it takes time to connect with your plants/animals. So, spend more time in your garden, talk to your plants or animals, learn how they are doing, know what's happening, see if you need to do anything for them, or simply enjoy the beauty.

5. At school, you can start with a cooking class before gardening because it's an activity that most kids like. It allows them to enjoy the food they cook. Through cooking, children can learn more about the ingredients and where they come from. They can also learn how to grow plant-based ingredients, etc. From there, you can continue growing an edible garden with your students.

6. Students will naturally be learning science, literacy, math, communication, teamwork, entrepreneurship, meditation, and many more skills through interaction with nature and cooking. Allow this process to unfold uniquely for each student.

7. Learn about your area or country's local or indigenous plants with the students and connect with local farmers or businesses.

8. Involve any experts in your community. For example, there might be parents willing to share their expertise in food and gardening with you and your students. There might also be nearby permaculture gardens or organizations on regenerative farming. Bring your students to visit these places or invite representatives to your school.

9. Reflect, learn, and evolve as you go. Enjoy the process.

"The freedom to play is one of the most meaningful gifts we can give our children."

~ Danielle Hayes

CHAPTER SIX

Healing From Within: Learning Through Safety and Connection

By Danielle Hayes

"When you connect to the heart of a child, anything is possible."

- Dr. Karyn Purvis

Mike's[6] fist thumped loudly on his desk, reverberating throughout the room. We all jumped at the sound. I felt my heartbeat quickening, knowing what was to come. Before I had time to consider my next move, Mike shoved his chair aside, and it crashed noisily to the floor as his body lunged toward the door. Ten sets of eyes were watching me; they all knew the drill. Mike ran from the classroom, slamming the door, windows rattling. We all breathed a sigh of relief once Mike was outside the room.

The above scenario is played out in many classrooms daily. An emotionally dysregulated child launching into a fight or flight response or, in Mike's case, a combined fight AND

---

6 Please note that any identifiable features have been changed to maintain confidentiality of all characters.

flight response. As a teacher, I felt torn; I had to ensure all of the children in my class were safe, but I also had Mike to consider. Fortunately, Mike and I had been working together for a while on his ability to regulate his emotions. He had come a long way, and leaving the classroom like this was a negotiated strategy. First, I knew I would find Mike outside the classroom, sitting on the stairs, doing his breathing techniques to calm his autonomic nervous system. Then, he would return to the class and continue learning.

Safety and Connection

Two things matter more than anything else to our nervous systems: safety and connection. Mike was fortunate; he was in a class of ten children with two teachers. I could 'tag team' with my co-teacher when Mike needed me to sit with him and support him to become regulated again. Our nervous systems communicate with each other, and a child in a state of fight or flight, as Mike was on that day, needs an emotionally stable adult around them to support a shift in their state. This support is known as co-regulation.

Having the time available to sit near Mike, doing my deep breathing to self-regulate my nervous system (which was always a little rattled after one of Mike's 'moment's) meant that Mike could soothe himself and move out of his survival state, allowing reflection and learning to happen again. Only then would Mike be able to express that he regretted what had happened and how he felt embarrassed that his peers had seen him like that again. Mike was able to walk back through the incident, noting what it felt like in his body when he knew he was in a state of fight or flight, reflecting on how he had followed the strategy of leaving the room and sitting on the stairs so that I knew he was safe. Mike was learning (albeit slowly) that he was not a 'naughty kid.' He just had a nervous system that reacted to certain stimuli, and he could regulate his emotions through connection and safety. More importantly, he practiced self-compassion for his humanness.

Traditionally, in the schooling system, Mike would be given a consequence, such as a 'time out' or detention, for his behavior, adding to a commonly held belief that Mike could control his emotions at that moment. However, science shows us that, when our autonomic nervous system launches into an activated state of survival, we cannot access the logical and rational areas of the brain, making a sensible choice almost impossible.

Shifting The Lens

Recent advances in neuroscience have created a shift in thinking about children's behaviors. I'm particularly interested in the work of *Dr. Mona Delahooke*,[7] who has simplified the concept of the *Polyvagal Theory by Dr. Stephen Porges*[8] into something tangible that teachers, parents, and therapists can apply. Understanding how our autonomic nervous system works and using that knowledge to support children has been one of the most enriching experiences of my career.

When we view a child through a behavior lens, we tend to believe a child is choosing the behavior to create a specific outcome (a 'top-down behavior'.) When we can shift the focus to viewing through a nervous system lens (an automatic internal reaction to an event: a 'bottom-up behavior',) we

7   https://monadelahooke.com/
8   https://www.stephenporges.com/

have an opportunity to connect. Instead of asking, "What is wrong with this child?" we can reframe this to, "What is this child trying to communicate?" We now have valuable information to help us support the child rather than just trying to control the child's behavior.

The Pathways

I believe it's essential to have a basic understanding of our autonomic nervous system. This has possibly been the most valuable thing I've learned in over thirty years of working with children and adolescents. It has supported my belief that humans do their best with their resources at any given time. Nevertheless, we have this incredibly advanced internal system that we must befriend and understand.

Our nervous systems have three pathways, to which Dr. Delahooke has kindly applied color characterizations, making it easy to teach to children.

Green Pathway (Social Engagement) - when we are on our Green Pathway, our body will feel relaxed, our muscles will be untensed and move with ease, our eyes can make contact with others, our face will be smiling, and our voice can adapt and match the situation we are in (e.g., quiet in a relaxed place or laughing with friends.) In this pathway, we can engage with others and be comfortable with time alone. We do not need to be constantly 'happy' on this pathway, but we can fully experience joy and fulfillment when it occurs. The Green Pathway provides a healthy sense of self, knowing that we can handle whatever arises through access to the top-level parts of our brain that help with problem-solving, organization, and critical thinking.

Red Pathway (Sympathetic Nervous System) - this is our Fight or Flight response, our survival mode. On this pathway, we are on high alert: muscles are tense, our eyes may dart around looking for signs of threat, our face frowns, and our jaw is clenched. On this pathway, the body prepares us to fight or escape a threat, so the action-based hormone adrenaline is pumped around the body, causing the body to move. This leads to jumpiness, yelling, hitting, kicking, running, hiding, or any number of big movements. I believe we need to understand this is an ancient response to a threat - our primitive ancestors spent much of their time on their Red Pathway and constantly feared being eaten by large creatures with big teeth. The challenge for our children today is that they are bombarded with age-inappropriate information (threats) at their fingertips, as well as toxic busyness, and the body reacts to the information the same way that our ancestors would have via the Red Pathway - fight or flight. This pathway is essential to our survival; however, staying on this pathway for long periods can impact our health, contributing to issues such as anxiety and autoimmune conditions. It also has a significant impact on our capacity to learn new things.

Blue Pathway (Freeze Zone) - this is our shutdown response. Historically, if the fight or flight response had not worked and the huge creature with big teeth was about to devour our cave-person, the nervous system cleverly developed an adaptation to shut down, or freeze, feelings of emotional or physical pain. Also known as dissociation, a child on this pathway may appear lethargic, sad, glassy-eyed, disengaged, compliant, and slow. The child may be unable to communicate verbally, as access to the speech and language areas of the brain has been disconnected.

Children in a frozen state are often labeled 'lazy,' as they cannot try anything new on this pathway, nor do they have the energy to engage with others.

While the above information is a very simplistic explanation of the nervous system, the goal is for our children to become emotionally flexible and build the skills to adapt their pathway in the required situation. While we all share the same three pathways physiologically, each pathway is shaped by our own unique experiences. To build resilience, we all need to understand how our nervous system responds to specific things, ranging from sensory experiences (smells, tastes, sounds, movement, textures, etc.) to physical and emotional experiences. Our nervous system is as unique as we are and shapes how we behave in any situation.

Offering: Spend a couple of moments checking in with yourself right now. What cues is your body giving you as to your current pathway? Notice your heartbeat - is it fast or slow or somewhere in between? Notice if your body is easily sitting still, or does it need to keep moving, even in small ways? Notice your breathing - is it shallow and based on the area of your lungs, or are you breathing deeper into your belly? What pathway do you feel you are on right at this moment? If you identify with the Red or Blue Pathways, take a moment to try and shift your pathway back to Green - breathe in slowly through your nose for the count of three and exhale very slowly through your mouth for the count of six, extending this even longer if you can. Two to three minutes of long exhale breathing is often enough to be able to switch on the relaxation response in our bodies, moving us closer to our Green Pathway.

Aligning My Values

My journey from educator to holistic therapist began before I left the classroom. Before working in a holistic school in Bali, Indonesia for four years, where we were incredibly blessed with small classes and two teachers per class, I had been teaching in a large, religious-based boy's school. This school had many boys who had arrived in Australia as refugees. As I observed their assimilation into our school, I saw these young men express extreme anger, deep sadness, pure determination, heartfelt compassion, and frustration through their behavior. Attempting to achieve the academic standards expected by the school while also needing to process deep trauma was fascinating and concerning for me to observe. I realized that, even after many years of working with children and teens, I needed to learn more about trauma and how to support our students, thus beginning the journey to becoming a therapist.

As I worked through my studies, I became intrigued with learning more about the nervous system and its impact on behavior. As I began closely observing what was happening to our children, it became apparent that, when a child 'misbehaved,' it almost always came from a shift in their nervous system pathway, from regulation (green) to dysregulation (red or blue), rather than being a conscious 'top down' choice. Everything changed for me when I shifted my perception from seeing the child through their behavior to seeing the child through a nervous system lens. I finally realized that working in a behavior-based education system focused on compliance didn't align with my values and beliefs about humans and how we develop and learn. When we focus on compliance, we cause the suppression of emotion

115

and the opportunity to learn about our emotional states. I believe that emotional awareness and a healthy, flexible nervous system are vital to creating healthy relationships with ourselves and others. Most importantly, I learned that, to develop emotional regulation, a child needs safety and connection. Unfortunately, in a traditional, industrialized school system, these essential components of emotional development are becoming more challenging to provide.

I must emphasize that I, in no way, blame my disillusionment with the traditional education system on our teachers and school leaders. The demands faced by our educators are unrealistic and unsustainable. How can these dedicated individuals provide safety and connection for our kids when they are under so much pressure themselves? I believe the system is broken, and it is the system that must change if we are to see children grow and develop into adults that possess a healthy sense of self.

Through the Therapist Lens

As a holistic therapist, I am passionate and excited about the tangible change I see occurring with the children I work with. I now have the privilege of working individually with children and families to support them in healing from trauma and learning to thrive in an often harsh and unpredictable world, pushing us more and more onto our Red or Blue Pathways. The theme of safety and connection is the basis of all my work. This holistic approach to healing creates a safe space and a trusted relationship between the therapist and the child. When a child feels safe and connected, they become open to learning, and together, we can build the skills needed to shift pathways. It's not my role to force a child to change their pathway (think behavior management). It is, however, my role to provide opportunities that allow a child to express what they need to express, in whatever format they need, and to build their skills of emotional flexibility. We are a team, and they are never alone, always supported. Together, we create a healing space around the child where they feel safe enough to dig deep within themselves, tapping into their ancient wisdom and exploring what they already often know about themselves but, for whatever reason, had suppressed.

I cannot explain the absolute joy of witnessing a child or adolescent begin to understand, accept, and love themselves for who they are. Building the skills of resilience, compassion, empathy, gratitude, and mindfulness is much easier when a child is open to learning and growing within themselves. Once that Green Pathway is discovered, it feels terrific, and they will want to keep returning to this state. I've seen children smile for the first time after months of sessions together, but it needed to be when they were ready to feel it.

If only we could support those in charge of our education systems to understand how the nervous system works and its connection to behavior and learning. If we want children to learn to their full capacity, we must allow opportunities for the child's brain to develop naturally - from the bottom up. When a child feels safe, connected, and secure, the brain's top levels are activated, allowing optimal learning to occur. Placing increasing academic pressure on young children ultimately has the opposite effect on both learning and emotional development. I now call this 'developmental abuse,' as it disrupts and inhibits our very cleverly designed developmental process. In the new education paradigm, the decision-makers, leaders, and co-creators will prioritize our children's mental health and wellbeing, acknowledging this essential component of a connected and healthy society.

I support children in their healing journey through various therapy styles in my practice but always from a 'bottom-up' approach. Safety and connection first, learning and strategies second. Each child/teen is free to choose what works best for them at that moment. They have the chance to access art and creativity, play, yoga, sand tray, talk therapy, relaxation, and mindfulness, with psychoeducation woven throughout each session as required.

Psychoeducation is where children learn specifically about their nervous system, their brains, and their bodies and how they are connected to what they have been experiencing. Once children feel safe and open to learning, they are incredibly curious and eager to learn all they can about their minds and bodies.

Here are some stories that demonstrate the power of a child healing themselves once they feel that sense of safety and connection.

The Power of Play

"Enter into children's play and you will find the place where their minds, hearts, and souls meet."

- Virginia Axline

The freedom to play is one of the most meaningful gifts we can give our children. Play is a fully embodied experience in which children use their imaginations, opening their minds to their full learning potential. Through play, they learn to 'listen in' to what their inner voice tells them and how to express themselves fully and freely. In addition, play provides opportunities for children to navigate their Green, Red, and Blue Pathways naturally, allowing them to build crucial skills in emotional flexibility.

I'm always in awe watching children play. I've observed children using play to express extreme joy, sadness, anger, and frustration. In a therapeutic setting, child-centered play provides an effective and much-needed opportunity for children to express themselves openly, aligning with my belief that children can tap into their inner wisdom and heal themselves with the proper support. Of course, while patterns emerge in children's play, each child's experience will be as individual as they are. Nevertheless, play is an essential developmental experience that should be at the core of all educational systems or pathways.

Cailen's Story: Three-year-old Cailen came to visit me in my therapy playroom, as he was having difficulty accepting that his parents had recently brought a new baby into the home. Cailen was hostile, even aggressive, toward his baby sister, displaying dysregulated behaviors, particularly in the evenings. *Child-Centered Play Therapy* is a form of therapy that provides a child with a safe space to play with carefully selected toys. During the session, my role is to observe and only join the play when the child initiates it, creating a space for co-regulation and safety. During Cailen's first session, he found one of the baby dolls and dragged it around the room, using the bottle to smack the baby in the face. Cailen spoke angrily to the baby doll, yelling loudly at it and trying to force it to drink.

If a child displayed this behavior at school, we would probably intervene and speak to the child about treating each other with kindness and respect. However, Cailen needed to express in the only way he knew how that his world had been turned upside-down when this new baby came into the house. Cailen expressed through his play that evening meal times had become very stressful in the household, and he missed the old times when his parents had more time to spend with him over dinner. All the stress in the home in the evening didn't feel as safe for him, and his autonomic nervous system responded with anger and sadness (his fight response.)

After a couple of sessions where Cailen beat up the baby doll and had a conversation between myself and his parents about readjusting what was happening at mealtimes, Cailen started to play very differently with the baby doll, showing empathy and care by gently feeding the doll with the bottle. Mum and dad reported that Cailen had become far more gentle with his baby sister, and as time passed, Cailen is now a proud big brother who adores his little sister. Cailen had some unresolved emotions that he needed to express in a safe, coregulated space. Play can reveal much about what a child needs to express or communicate.

Offering: Connected Play - create a time and space to play where your child is in charge (safety considered, of course). If it feels comfortable, allow your child to direct you and organize the play on their terms. If possible, try not to correct them or redirect them.

- What type of play do they initiate?

- Can they take the initiative during the play, or are they constantly asking you for direction or approval?

- If your child asks, "What do you think about...?" try answering with, "Hmmm, I'm wondering what you think about it."

- If they ask, "Do you like this?" (in relation to a picture they have drawn, or a tower they have built, etc.), try answering, "It's more important for you to decide if you like it or not. What are your thoughts?"

Allowing a child to be in charge for an amount of time during play gives the child a chance to feel in control. This builds a sense of self-efficacy, which is the feeling of, "I can do this," as well as letting your child know that you value their opinion.

Movement To Discover

"Yoga is the perfect opportunity to be curious about who you are."

- Jason Crandell

A child with a healthy nervous system will be able to identify and manage what they are feeling via the cues from their body. They will possess a healthy sense of self, and a strong connection between their brain and body will develop, known as brain-body integration. Unfortunately, in the therapy sessions I run, I'm seeing increasing numbers of children who are unable to identify a basic feeling within the body, such as, "I'm feeling hot or cold," "I'm feeling hungry or full," "I'm feeling sad or lonely" or "I need to use the toilet." The sense that allows us to tap into what's happening internally is called 'interoception,' and it is something that I genuinely believe we need to support our children to develop as early as possible. An underdeveloped sense of interoception means that children cannot identify a cue that the body provides (such as the feeling of a full bladder or butterflies in the tummy) and then decide what to do with that cue. This can lead to emotional disconnect, meltdowns, undereating, overeating, and toileting accidents, to name a few. A strong sense of interoception for teens will allow them to notice if something doesn't feel right for them, hopefully deciding not to get into the car with the driver who has been drinking or not to take that pill just because everyone else is. Interoception challenges are widespread in children who have been diagnosed with ADHD, Autism, and with those who have experienced trauma.

For many children and teens today, their lives have become overly sedentary. They are expected to sit for long periods each day at school and after school. They sit still for many hours playing online games, watching videos, or accessing social media. As a result, their developing bodies are under-stimulated. There is a belief that, when a child is sitting in stillness, they are being 'good' (meaning compliant). However, when it comes time to finish their game, they display bottom-up behaviors that can last for hours.

Many parents remain unaware that, while a child's body may appear relatively still during gaming, their mind is on high alert. Many games involve the need to make quick decisions, life and death, violence and aggression, and this stimulates a child's state of fight or flight internally. The extra adrenaline flowing into the body during gaming time needs to be released through movement, but the child is not identifying the cues it provides. When asked to finish their game (to come and have dinner, for example), the flood of adrenaline takes over, and the child can lose all control, spiraling into a highly activated state. There is a disconnect between their body and mind.

I have found that a valuable way to connect a child with their mind and body is through yoga. Yoga is a fun, healthy, and effective way to develop a child's sense of interoception. We often perceive yoga as being about calm, slow movements, but in a therapeutic sense, children's yoga is quite active. Of course, the component of relaxation to finish a session is essential in helping a child notice their state shifting from activated (red) to relaxed (green.)

In a therapeutic yoga session, I support a child to build that sense of brain/body connection through various movements. I will sometimes ask a child to hold a pose for thirty seconds to see if they can identify which parts of the body they can feel and which parts are changing as they hold the pose. They are often intrigued by the number of muscles involved in a single pose. They notice what happens to those muscles when they release a pose. They begin to notice when they are feeling silly, having fun, or starting to feel bored or annoyed. I deliberately create situations to explore various feelings, as we want children to know that all feelings are acceptable and necessary. We must listen to our feeling and decide what we do. Can we sit with it, as we know it will pass? Or, do we heed the feeling and remove ourselves from the situation? In our western society, we are adept at pushing away uncomfortable feelings and grasping onto the more positive emotions. Ultimately, yoga allows us to notice all feelings and be OK with them while listening to the messages we receive about ourselves and our place in the world. It builds a sense of self and allows us to work through feelings of insecurity by realizing that we don't have to master everything straightaway and it is normal to feel uncomfortable sometimes.

Children usually respond well to science, so, in a yoga/ interoception session, I often use a heart rate monitor to help a child understand what is happening in their bodies when they have been moving and then notice the difference when they are still. They are always surprised at how quickly their heart rate drops during a short relaxation or breathing exercise. When we connect the feeling of increased heart activity with the sense of fight or flight, they start to notice the body cues when they feel stressed, nervous, or overwhelmed. This awareness is the beginning of the development of interoception.

Rebecca's Story: Nine-year-old Rebecca could not answer a question as basic as, "What's one good thing that has happened this week?" I asked this same question month after month at the beginning of our sessions. It wasn't that Rebecca never experienced anything positive, but she was unable to identify anything that FELT good to her. I kept asking because I knew her answer would eventually change after our work together through yoga and movement. That would be my first clue to the shift in her internal state, with the brain and body building a healthy connection.

At the beginning of each session, Rebecca would immediately get the balance board and stand on it. She couldn't express why she needed it, but her body instinctively knew what she had to do to regulate herself. Rebecca needed balance and movement to soothe her nervous system and feel safe and connected. After several months of therapy, incorporating yoga and movement, Rebecca drew me a picture that spoke volumes of what she was experiencing internally. The drawing was a stick figure person, lying on its side, with its head wholly separated from the body. Rebecca could not express verbally what she had been experiencing all these years. Still, her drawing showed that she was starting to become aware that she had an underdeveloped sense of interoception, which was a starting point for her understanding of why we practiced yoga and movement together. From this point, Rebecca engaged more in her yoga and movement activities and began expressing feelings of joy, sadness, and frustration. This certainly didn't solve all Rebecca's challenges. However, when she started to feel into her body, she was able to begin to take charge of her responses to different situations.

Offering: Take time to observe your child while gaming or on a device. Notice when they begin to fidget, tap their hands or feet, if their leg starts moving up and down, or if they start rocking or rolling their body. Notice this in yourself when you are at work, on the computer, or on the phone for too long. When adrenaline builds, it creates an involuntary movement in the body of which we are often unaware of. Encourage your child to take regular movement breaks to support emotional regulation and release stress. Make sure you have some too!

Getting Creative

"Art can permeate the deepest part of us, where no words exist."

- Eileen Miller, The Girl Who Spoke with Pictures: Autism Through Art.

For children who have experienced trauma, finding words to connect with feelings can be very challenging. Children often experience a Blue Pathway (freeze state) response to painful emotions and memories. Therefore, it is essential to provide spaces of safety and connection for our children to feel free to express what they need to express.

My therapy room always has a pad of paper and a bucket of art supplies close by. When I encounter a child or teen on their Blue Pathway, I often place some creative items on the table in front of them. I then sit quietly, letting them know I am there, co-regulating with them until they can come back into their bodies. Often, even after shifting out of their Blue Pathway, a child still cannot verbalize what happened. They know that they are welcome to use the paper for whatever they need to at that moment. Some will scribble on the page or draw lines, often in carefully chosen colors, to express deep anger, sadness, frustration, or resentment. Others will draw themselves in a specific situation or with a particular person. I have seen a child draw a very thick line down the center of the page, with their family on one side and themself alone on the other. Other children write in a frenzied way, releasing a gush of words that had been sitting internally for some time. Sometimes, they will read their words aloud, sharing their pain with me. Occasionally, they will tear it up into little pieces, releasing the emotion with every rip of the paper. It doesn't matter what option they choose, as long as it feels right. They know what they need to do. Mike, the child from the beginning of this chapter, once drew himself sitting outside the classroom, looking calm and relaxed amongst the trees. This was how we established that he needed to leave the classroom to be able to regulate and return to his Green Pathway. The power of a picture!

Offering: If you or a child you know is experiencing anxiety, this activity is often beneficial. It can also be done with someone experiencing anger, frustration, loneliness, etc. Prepare some paper and colored markers. Now, close your eyes and feel into your anxious feelings for a moment. If that is too difficult, think of a time when you felt anxious. Notice what happens in your body when you think about it. Try to sit with these feelings for a moment or two, noticing any signs of discomfort in the body. Now, open your eyes and choose a color that would describe it.

Remember this is art, and there is no right or wrong. It's whatever you feel works for you. Now, choose a shape that best describes your anxious feelings and begin using your selected colored marker to create the form on the page. I've seen children scribble everywhere, sharing the chaotic and out-of-control feelings that anxiety often creates. I've seen children draw block-type shapes with thick lines, creating something that shows how much it feels like their anxiety controls them.

On the other hand, I've witnessed soft, sad-like, gentle shapes being created. There's no right or wrong - whatever shows up for you is perfect! If your mind starts to judge your creation, take a deep breath, letting go of all self-criticism. Once you have created something on the page, take a different colored marker (one that will stand out) and give your creation some human features, such as eyes, nose, mouth, arms, legs, etc. Turn it into a character. Now, give your newly created character a name (mine is called Anxious Annie, but she's well-known to me simply as 'Annie'.) Suddenly, our anxious thoughts are not just inside us but something tangible that we can look at and chat to. Rather than being something that controls us, we can now have a chat with our little friend when we are feeling overwhelmed with anxious thoughts, saying something along the lines of, "Thank you, Annie, for trying to look after me. I appreciate your help, but I'm OK. I can do this on my own." This gives a sense of control back to the child. The character becomes like a friend trying to help, but the child can take some action to regain that feeling of being in control.

Beyond The Child

As much as it brings me incredible joy and gratitude to connect with children and teens and witness their unique and powerful journeys, some of the most rewarding times for me are through the connections with parents and teachers. Supporting our parents and educators to explore and discover their nervous system pathways leads to growth in co-regulation skills and increased emotional support for our children. Every adult in a child's life who develops these skills has the opportunity to change the life of a child in the most profound way. When I left teaching several years ago, I felt deflated and disheartened at the system. The truth is, I still am. In my opinion, the system has let down our educators, our children, and our parents. However, I witness daily the willingness of the parents and educators to sow the seeds of a new paradigm of education through their personal growth and the support of their children and students through awareness, connection, and action.

I have been on my healing journey since I left teaching, and I'm truly blessed and grateful to learn something about myself through every interaction. I am excited and humbled to be part of every child's healing, of coming back to knowing and self-love. The teachers, parents, and most importantly, the children and teens I have the privilege of connecting with bring me hope, hope that our world will be OK. I genuinely believe the emotional future of our children will be born from wisdom and passion for seeing their internal worlds thrive, to give them the tools to be the best humans they can be. If we can provide our children with safety and connection, we know they have everything they need to flourish: loving themselves and others, taking care of our world into the future, and contributing to a compassionate and caring society.

A message from the SOVEREIGN student rising….

"I am here to honor my unique song!"

"I am here to learn what lights me up!"

"I am here to follow my own true excitement!"

~ Clare Ford

CHAPTER SEVEN

THE RISE OF THE EDUPRENEUR

By Clare Ford
(Academic Coach and Teen Mentor)

As we know, severe educational gaps are not addressed by the current outdated system or the "old" paradigm. As a result, children are more anxious, depressed, and suicidal than ever. Parents are floundering, and young people's emotional and spiritual growth needs addressing.

I am passionate about transforming the face of education and its very foundation. Unfortunately, the one-size-fits-all approach is failing our children now more than ever, and they are not adequately prepared with the transferable skills they need to support them in adulthood.

My vision is to create a global-leading education platform that will be the gold standard for learning and valuing emotional well-being, personal development, and spiritual growth to support academic success. The key reason is to potentialize the next generation by enabling them to become fully self-expressed.

Why are edupreneurs a different breed of teachers?

Edupreneurs are passionate, skilled, experienced teachers who have chosen to step out of the classroom and build their own educational business. Like me, many are bringing their passion for teaching and supporting students, along with their teaching skillset – and a whole lot more - to the table.

I have 20 years of experience in the education sector, working with children and families from culturally diverse backgrounds in various school settings worldwide. I have also been a school governor, designated safeguarding officer, ethnic minority achievement strategy coordinator, and literacy coordinator. I have supported children and teens with special education learning needs, including dyslexia, dyspraxia, ADHD, ASD, EAL, and ESL. Not that these labels are relevant anymore, as we are here to dissolve separation as we move into oneness consciousness.

I am a divorced mum with two teen sons and have spent some years co-parenting while building a business and running a home. So, I fully understand the ups and downs of parenting, raising teens (and all the angst that goes with that,) and the pressures that teachers, educators, homeschoolers, and the senior leadership team face.

As a business owner, I have developed a range of skills that require me to grow as a person and navigate the ups and downs of being an entrepreneur, especially during a worldwide pandemic. Discipline, resourcefulness, investment, stepping outside my comfort zone, and learning new skills enables me to relate to my students' feelings authentically.

132

I can model personal growth with them and relate anecdotes of how my failures led to success, how I had to persevere to get something right, how I tried something new, and how it did or didn't work out for me.

I can talk to my teen clients about different ways of doing things: the different lifestyles that digital nomads lead, world-schooling opportunities, investment ideas, passive income, and how you can sell digital products in your sleep. It is so crucial that young people realize **there are alternatives!**

I also teach students how to stay healthy, physically, mentally, emotionally, and spiritually, by giving students strategies to manage exam stress, for example, or how to manage their time effectively when it comes to revision. More importantly, I can help them to explore what they are drawn to. I teach children about crystals, meditation, journaling, moon cycles and biorhythms, hormones and sleep patterns, and values and boundaries.

Sometimes these topics are courses in their own right, sometimes they are a lesson as part of a bigger program, and sometimes they are a tangential conversation. It doesn't matter. As a Reiki Master and Quantum Energy Healer, I follow my intuition and tap into what is needed in the moment to help the student feel supported, heard, and guided. This is the freedom and magic of teaching that educates, empowers, and elevates both student and educator.

I am also passionate about conscious parenting approaches and how we, as parents and critical educators, need to work on ourselves to support and model emotional, spiritual, and intellectual growth for our children.

THE RISE OF THE DISCERNING PARENT

The parental conundrum

Parents can no longer bury their heads in the sand and pass on the responsibility for their child's learning to the school. The pandemic has helped us realize how inadequate mainstream schooling is and that we, the parents, are our child's best educators. Therefore, it's okay to outsource, ask for help, and delegate for our children to build on their natural strengths, gifts, talents, and attributes. After all, we adults have our strengths, weaknesses, and areas of expertise.

If children disengage or "switch off," the opportunity to learn critical skills is lost, putting that child at a disadvantage as a lifelong learner.

The parents I work with want their child or teen to find the path that is right for them, whether it's going to university, starting an apprenticeship, or building their own business, regardless of societal norms or family pressures.

I believe that conscious, aspirational parents have a pivotal and crucial role in the rise of the *new paradigm of education* since they know what is best for their child and are intuitively connected at a far deeper level than a class teacher. Perhaps, it is simply a case of permitting parents to step up and into the role of educator that is required. In light of the pandemic, there has been an incredible transformation in different types of schooling available to the discerning parent, so that we no longer focus only on league tables and catchment areas but can widen, broaden, and deepen exciting educational experiences for our children. I have interviewed experts and parents on the merits of homeschooling, flexi-schooling, world schooling, no schooling, forest schooling, democratic schooling, private schooling, public schooling, boarding schooling, and grammar schooling.

I am not advocating any particular type of schooling, just that parents carefully consider their lifestyle, values, culture, and long-term plans, so that their children thrive in the now and prepare for future successes.

What does it mean to discern?

That we learn from mistakes in order to rise...

The discerning parents know, intuitively, deep down in every cell of their being that now is the right time to break those generational patterns, the people-pleasing, and toeing the line; that it's okay to say no – to grandparents, to societal norms, to the crumbling and outdated education system.

Parents I speak with daily want to work with someone they can trust, who knows the education system and can take what works (minimal, in my humble opinion) and adapt what doesn't to fit the educational and emotional needs of each of their wonderfully unique children, so that confidence, resilience, and self-esteem are built through trust and progression. They want their child to be a happy, contented, engaged, life-long learner, curious about the world and unlocking their uniqueness and creativity while building the critical foundational skills to enable them to live a fully potentialized life as an adult.

The power of presence and perspicacity

Research and experience suggests that raising happy, healthy kids requires parents to do just one key thing. It's not about reading all the parenting bestsellers or signing your kids up for lots of extra-curricular activities. You don't even have to know precisely what you're doing, and you don't need a Ph.D. in education. Instead, you just have to show up and **connect.**

Showing up means bringing your whole being, your attention and awareness, into this moment with your child. We must be mentally and emotionally present for our children when we show up.

Propelling children through middle and high school, loading them with extra-curricular activities and hours of homework to push through a rigorous school curriculum towards the highest level of achievement is simply setting them up for disaster. That is the old paradigm of education and let's be honest – how many of us has that worked for?

The point is to develop an attitude of curiosity rather than immediate judgment.

Let us courageously and boldly teach a more balanced approach and encourage kids and teens to foster an individualized definition of success.

Finding schools, colleges, and universities that are a good fit and accepting that getting anything less than nine A*s is okay will do more to boost confidence and lessen anxiety for our teens.

It requires a dramatic leap of faith to trust that your teen can discover their own path if we give them the space to do so.

Therefore, it is imperative to parent children consciously from a young age to build those foundations and key life skills for later, helping them to become emotionally literate by developing social and emotional skills and regulation, nurturing a curious and enquiring mind, and fostering creative approaches to problem-solving.

Through this process, young people build confidence, resilience, resourcefulness, and self-esteem. They start to work hard and "show up" for themselves. They become intrinsically motivated and will do what it takes to move towards their goals. How do I know? Because I mentor teens to **discover their path**.

THE RISE OF THE SOVEREIGN STUDENT

What does it mean to be a sovereign student?

When "being sovereign," we possess our supreme or ultimate power.

Sovereignty implies that the individual is free and has the authority to conduct their own affairs.

A sovereign student will state,

"I am here to honor my unique song!"

"I am here to learn what lights me up!"

"I am here to follow my own true excitement!"

So how does this relate to education?

Firstly, lessons and learning are co-created with students and teachers. The inquiry is child-led, with the teacher simply acting as a guide or a "way-shower."

At Switched**ON!** we adopt a shoulder-to-shoulder approach to educational coaching and personal development. We are not at the front of the class, simply feeding information to our students. Instead, we are next to them, facilitating transformation. We encourage independent and critical thinking, foster curiosity, and empower young leaders to go beyond what they (and their parents) thought possible. We use a range of growth mindset techniques to enable children and teens to see that mistakes are stepping stones to greatness. We talk about comfort zones, boundaries, perseverance and resilience, procrastination and overwhelm, and everything in between.

How can you have a sovereign student in a group setting?

It's actually quite simple. We allow each other to dance to different tunes in a unified field, feeling safe to be uniquely seen, heard, and validated in a collective bubble. This is how we are rising toward a collective consciousness or, in simple terms, making a change from where we are now to a new awakened way of living.

Let's see how this works practically in an online classroom setting.

THE NEW PARADIGM OF EDUCATION – IN ACTION!

The Switched**ON! Learning Method** ™ uses three core pillars, the three C's: clarity, curiosity, and collaboration, to ensure that learners become high-level thinkers, enabling them to untap their potential and achieve more than they ever thought possible. Let's consider each pillar.

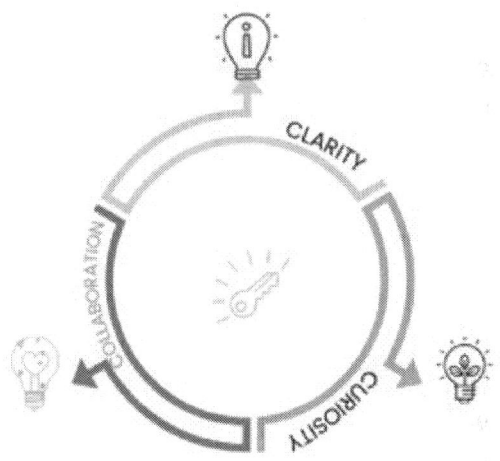

PILLAR ONE: CLARITY

This is the critical pre-working and planning phase on which everything else hinges...

"If you fail to plan, you are planning to fail."

~ Benjamin Franklin

At Switched**ON!**, students gain clarity in the following four areas, so that they are intrinsically motivated to learn, exponentially increasing their likelihood of success:

1. Clear Purpose - their WHY

2. Clear Vision - their WHAT

3. Clear Goals - their HOW

4. Winner's Mindset - their FUEL

Note: it is **their** purpose, vision, and goals, not outcomes dictated to them by a government curriculum, school, teacher, or parent.

Let's take **creative writing** as an example to demonstrate how to use this pillar:

Most students start writing their stories without deciding how they will end. As a result, here's what happens: they go off on tangents, bring in more problems or new characters, over-complicate the plot, and often never get around to finishing their story.

It's like heading off on a road trip without a clear destination in mind and then just going wherever you fancy without ever reaching your endpoint.

So, here is what the learner can focus on instead:

By planning their story out in five clear sections before writing it, the learner can "start with the destination in mind," making their story hang together better. The story needs to have a (1) beginning, (2) rising action, (3) climax, (4) falling action, and (5) resolution.

Planning is useful because it supports learners to clear their thoughts before they start writing, saving them valuable time later on, as they will know exactly what to write about and what comes next, just like having a Sat Nav to take you where you want to go, without worrying about getting lost and losing time along the way.

So, the first thing that will help learners write proficiently is to work on having a **clear** plan and story structure.

PILLAR TWO: CURIOSITY

Encouraging high-level questioning and critical thinking to produce high-quality work.

"Curiosity is the engine of achievement."

~ Ken Robinson

Students at SwitchedON! learn that the quality of their questions determines the quality of their answers. By encouraging curiosity, learners develop resourcefulness, persistence, resilience, and critical thinking skills in a nurturing learning environment where they feel safe to ask questions without fear of ridicule or public humiliation. These are the questions we consider:

1. WHAT ELSE?

2. HOW ELSE?

3. WHERE ELSE?

In our example with creative writing, many students give up quickly if they sense that they are not writing something that will please their teacher. This results in the use of the same vocabulary, sentence structures, and ideas because students know these are safe and will achieve an average to good mark and keep the teacher and parents off their backs! I know many children who are too scared to use higher-level vocabulary because they are afraid of misspelling words.

If you think about it, it's like only eating two or three meals you like and never being brave enough to try anything else. Instead, learners are encouraged to focus on asking themselves what else can I write? How else can I write it? Where else have I written it?

This form of questioning supports students to vary their vocabulary and sentence structure and challenges them to keep to their plan, so they create a coherent piece of writing.

Just like with food, children need a varied "buffet" of words and writing techniques to choose from to help invigorate their writing as they develop their skills and confidence around the use of language.

PILLAR THREE: COLLABORATION

Working with like-minded, driven, and aspirational students in a positive learning environment means certain success.

> *"Many ideas grow better when transplanted into another mind than the one where they sprang up."*

> **~ Oliver Wendell-Holmes**

At Switched**ON!,** we value community and connection. Parents, students, tutors, and coaches ensure that communication channels are open, so that learners are supported every step of the way. Here are the key considerations that we share for effective collaborations:

1. ESTABLISH YOUR "A" TEAM

2. TWO HEADS, ONE PROBLEM

3. CONSCIOUS COMMUNICATION

Most students try to figure things out on their own. They may be worried about looking stupid in front of their peers for admitting that they didn't know something. Even if group work is initiated in the classroom, it's not always effective due to large class sizes, noise levels, and disruptions.

As a result, their confidence plummets, and they feel less inclined to try when something feels challenging. They stick to what they know, and their learning and grades plateau. In short, they begin to switch off.

Would you try to climb Mount Everest on your own with a backpack that is only half-full of the equipment you are going to need?

Let's focus on developing the confidence, communication, listening, and leadership skills to work with others, share ideas, feedback, and knowledge, and empower our future leaders with the transferable skills and tools they require.

In our creative writing scenario, learners realize that they have great ideas, can make valuable contributions, and can help other students while graciously receiving help and feedback.

Like a mountain climber lending a helping hand to their friend to get over those final peaks.

To summarise, what makes my unique learning method such a game-changer in the classroom?

1. It is learner-led, making it relevant and meaningful to each individual student.

2. We value creativity, fun, and interaction.

3. It combines proven pedagogy with growth mindset hacks – academic coaching instead of simply tutoring or teaching.

4. We use flexible learning platforms that suit all learning styles, so both "fish" and "monkeys" succeed.

5. Learning is nurtured in a positive learning environment with aspirational learners.

I am passionate about seeing young people achieve something they didn't think they could do – making the impossible possible and seeing them shine.

For example, **our Little Authors' Big Ideas Creative Writing Quest** gets children from ages 7-14 to start with no idea and a blank piece of paper and then plan, write, edit, illustrate, and publish their own story in **just a week!**

We support children from all over the world with different backgrounds, abilities, and ideas and have a 100% success rate.

If you would like to access our free resources and training, chat with us further, or learn more about our courses to educate, empower and elevate your learner, visit our website at: www.switchedonglobal.com.

"Self-Directed Learning isn't only about learning. It's about life. Life is, after all, self-directed. Isn't it?"

~ Jeneen Gacek

CHAPTER EIGHT

Self-Directed Learning - In SEARCH of More

By Jeneen Gacek

"The Secret to change is to focus all your energy, not on fighting the old, but on building the new."

- Socrates.

We fell upon Self-Directed Learning by accident.

Our children at the time were 8 and 11 years old and attending an International Holistic school here in Bali, Indonesia. They walked free, often barefoot, and learned to grow vegetables in the community garden. Short moments in the day were dedicated to meditation along with their regular school subjects, and kids of all ages gathered in the mornings to connect. We were in a steady routine, waking up frantically rushed in the mornings, dashing around making lunches, flinging items into backpacks, and trying to coerce the kids into the car, each time hoping to stuff one last rolled-up pancake in their mouths before leaving, so they could survive until lunch. After school, we often picked up one child with empty eyes (who craved more excitement and challenge) and the other close to collapse from exhaustion (over-stimulation, I think). We continued to do it though, as all families did.

We thought, "This is normal, isn't it?" Both our children functioned well enough to get above-average grades. Every once in a while, I saw a glimmer of spark in their eyes. Our son, Java (11), was obsessed with creating a replica of an Antonov 225, the largest airplane from Ukraine. Our daughter Khiana (8) dreamed of going to London to see the Tower of London after learning about its torturous history. It felt like a fairly typical family existence.

My husband and I sat in the living room, staring out the window at the waving palm leaves. The smell of the leather couch was bold and intensified because the silence in the room was deafening. We sat facing each other, blankly, internally searching for a solution. We had been running a fashion accessories brand for almost fifteen years, but we knew it was time for a change. We didn't know where the changes would land us, but we craved more flexibility and freedom for our family.

I began the search for something to fit our new needs and fell upon a Self-Directed Learning program online. Something inside me came alive! Words like freedom, a journey of discovery, and a spark of curiosity lit my soul on fire. There was tingling energy that only surfaces when something connects with your inner knowing. It is like an electrical surge that rushes through your body. (Do you know the feeling?)

At dinner that night, we all sat down to talk about it. The consensus was that we were willing to try it for a year. I felt excited and nervous, knowing we were in for a wild ride.

It's been six years since we began, and it has, indeed, been a wild ride. What I have learned about myself, my family, and my children is both awe-inspiring and mind-blowing.

I would love to share what we have learned, as I think it's an important piece of the puzzle of the New Paradigm of Education. While the process of seeing education and learning in a new way was perplexing and personally challenging, I also became inquisitive and intrigued by the changes I witnessed in myself and my family. This has sparked a newfound interest that brings me here with you today.

For those that venture to try something outside of the traditional school system, it began as it does for most families. We brought school home. We created a schedule based on subjects and hourly increments. We had color-coded spreadsheets with everything listed for the week. Like school, we developed a plan for testing, projects, and presentations. We downloaded apps for science and math and had an endless list of reading and comprehension sheets. We got desks for the kids and created workstations in their rooms. I'm an organizer with a personal obsession with spreadsheets, so this all felt simple. We were going to nail it. I felt it.

Slowly, though, things started to fall apart. First, our children didn't want to sit at their desks; they wanted to sit on the floor or on their beds. "How will you focus if you don't sit at the desk?" I thought to myself, irritated and confused. It was only a few weeks until the schedules were no longer followed. They started to zone out and lose focus quickly. Each subject seemed to start or end with either yelling, tears, or both. I felt like the whole situation was beginning to spin out of control, and I couldn't hold things together. What was I doing wrong?

Thankfully, with our new Self-Directed Learning program, we had a Learning Consultant, whom we met with each week. Her goal was to help our family create a healthy environment for learning. She helped us to re-think and re-organize our schedule to be better suited for our family. More importantly, she helped us see a new way of approaching learning. It felt like what I confidently saw as black and white, was now a million shades of grey. I began to question everything. Should I force a child, crying and frustrated, to continue learning math? Should they sit at their desks to complete their work? Is there another way? Should we schedule subjects every hour to fit everything in during the week? Is it okay to spend 3-4 hours in the day creating characters and telling stories with Lego? Is going surfing in the morning considered learning? What time does a good schedule start? How do we know they are learning? What are the most important things to learn? How do we keep the love of learning in their eyes?

My belief system of rules and structure that held my life and business together was at risk of collapsing, and I was still trying desperately to keep it all together. Could it be that I suddenly questioned everything I believed to be accurate? The feeling of losing control was off the charts, and I started to lose confidence in what we were doing. I had only seen one way of learning: the traditional way. Could it be that a new path was possible?

This unfolded for years following these initial months. I let go of my conditioned beliefs to maintain a sense of sanity. I HAD TO. This is what unschooling is. It's letting go of previous beliefs and opening up to new ones. Slowly, we let go of schedules, subjects, and testing. We let go of expectations and proving our learning. Somewhere within me, though, was a deeper and stronger belief in people. The trust I felt wavered, week to week, but was enough for us to stay the course. We practiced following our learning instincts, understanding our patterns, observing our strengths and weaknesses, and experimenting with new ways of learning. We learned that my son loved taking things apart and putting them together better and faster. He loved efficiency, timed activities, and feeling challenged. He loved taking calculated risks. We learned that my daughter preferred vision boards over lists, continually created complex characters and stories, and could stay within a creative flow for hours. She loved writing, reading, and music.

One of the big obstacles in this process was other people. They waltzed in, wondering aloud as they witnessed our new family routine that lacked subjects, testing, classrooms, and schedules. I understood their questions because our life wasn't considered normal, but it was, quite honestly, a constant reminder of our choice to leap blindly off the cliff. It stirred up everything repeatedly, leading to a feeling of continuous turmoil.

Years passed, but what I've witnessed has taught me a lot about myself and our children and the learning process. As a result, I'm much more comfortable and confident with our evolving and changing patterns that are personalized for each family member. This has become clear to me through insightful moments throughout the journey, moments that I would have never witnessed had we not taken the opportunity to try something new.

This change allowed our children to become independent and self-aware of themselves and their bodies. They know how to manage their sleep and when their food choices affect their moods or productivity. They have a much deeper understanding of their character, tendencies, and motivations. They can acknowledge what lights them up, when to take inspired action, and when they need to step away. They are curious and love learning. We no longer have a school year. They learn all year round by choice. We have healthy conversations and respect each other's character and interests. We have connected deeply as a family because we had the time and space. I feel incredibly confident and trust in their ability to navigate life and learning and handle the challenges thrown their way with kindness and confidence.

"Self-Directed Learning isn't only about learning. It's about life. Life is, after all, self-directed. Isn't it?"

Self-Directed Learning means that the learner takes the initiative, sometimes on their own or with the help of others. They figure out what they want and need to learn. They define those goals, where or how to get the information, how to learn in a way that is best for them, and to determine the outcome or result of their efforts. It sounds like *life,* doesn't it?

I've created the SEARCH Philosophy for Learning based on our Self-Directed Journey. It outlines a spiral scaffolding of a process that our family has lived through and that changed the course of our lives.

As a human race, we have continued to develop and are always searching for better ways. This is evolution. The dictionary definition of evolution is the gradual development of something, especially from a simple to a more complex form. This is what we are doing. We have been moving from a simple life (think living in caves, hunting for food) to finding ways to navigate a more complex reality (the Internet,

AI, mental health, Global connection). I continue to search for ways to show up and support others in this New Paradigm as a parent, as a leader, and as a human.

When our Learning Journey started to fall apart, and I started to question everything, my biggest question was, "What IS the purpose?" Children spend twelve years in school preparing for life. What do we want them to learn? What is the end goal? How do we teach our children essential life skills? How do we prepare them for the future world? Is what they are learning preparing them?

These were the questions that I was asking myself. First, I needed to know what the priorities were. Second, I wanted to understand why we needed to learn what we were told to learn. I could no longer accept the truth I had been conditioned to believe. I needed to understand for myself.

Here starts the beginning of the SEARCH. SEARCH is an acronym that describes our family philosophy; **S**ense of Self, **E**xperimentation, **A**ction, **R**eflection, **C**hange, and **H**uman flourishing.

S stands for Sense of Self

Our Sense of Self is best described as our own perception of the characteristics that define our identity. It could be personality traits, abilities, our belief system, likes and dislikes, or the things that motivate us — these all contribute to our self-image. This is the development I have noticed most in our kids through this Self-Directed Learning process.

Not long after we started Self-Directed Learning, we began having a Weekly Family Meetup. As a family, this was our time to discuss and plan for the week. One Monday morning, I was eager to share new ideas with the kids.

I had been feeling quite good about where we were as a family, but I kept getting this gnawing feeling that it just wasn't enough. So, I continued searching for new activities and classes for the kids and couldn't wait to share what I had found.

One morning in our meeting, it came my turn to talk, and I jumped at the chance to describe the activities I had discovered. While revealing the juicy details, I glanced around at the others and saw their lights completely switched off. I stopped. 'What could be the problem?' I thought to myself.

I felt instantly annoyed. I had made all this effort and spent a lot of time gathering this information.

"What?!" I said, sounding a bit irritated (but quite honestly, trying to sound like a kind, curious parent.) I spoke calmly, "Do these not sound interesting to you? What do you guys want to do?"

We didn't get very far that morning. I left our meeting feeling down and discouraged. After some time had passed and the irritation subsided, I went to my daughter Khiana's room to talk. I asked her about the activities.

After much discussion, questions, and active listening, I had an insightful moment.

I realized a couple of important things. First, big groups were not her thing. We often assume that social interaction looks the same for all kids (and that school is the ultimate example), but different people have different preferences. Some thrive in large groups, while others prefer to work alone or in small, connected pods. She preferred 2-3 kids at most.

Second, even more importantly, I discovered that she needed to know the teacher or the mentor first. She needed to feel safe, confident, and connected with this person to give a hard YES to a new activity. Ah! Now her reaction made sense. She wasn't getting the information she needed to make the decision. It was only through active discussion and reflection that we were able to discover this and move forward.

At that moment, we decided that each time she would embark on a new activity, we would make an effort for her to meet the teacher and that she was entitled to follow her instincts in making the decision based on their connection. This understanding of herself (aka Sense of Self) has continued to serve her exploration during our learning journey, and I feel confident it will benefit her for life.

Now, looking back, I can see the importance of this. It is the foundation of our being and this philosophy. If a house is built on a poor foundation, we all know what happens to the house.

Over the long run, some cracks and shifts weaken it and can lead to long-term collapse. (Think of struggles with mental health, depression, anxiety, or burnout.)

Their deeper understanding of themselves guides our children through life. While continuing to build a strong sense of self, children build better relationships, have a better understanding of others, reach goals more easily, and ultimately, feel happier. This is what, I believe, should be the foundation of education and learning.

"To know thyself is the beginning of wisdom."

- Socrates

E stands for Experimentation

This Experimentation stage is about two different aspects: the mindset and the process of learning.

Mindset

Let's picture this. You hear about this beautiful campground destination from a friend.

You are fixated on this location for the weekend, so you map out the route and start the adventure with your family.

Next thing you know, you are faced with construction, and the road is closed. You get frustrated and angry that your family plans are ruined. You return home with many tears and anger from everyone about the collapsed plans.

Alternatively, let's say you were faced with construction and the road is closed. You **wonder** if there are other ways to reach the destination. You **re-visit** the map, seeing multiple roads that could take you there, possibly longer or windier, but you are **willing to try**. You start down this **new path** and notice many other gorgeous places you didn't know existed. You **see** a stunning waterfall and stop for a roadside picnic. The journey is glorious, and then, after a long, adventurous day, you reach the beautiful campground destination, just in time to catch the sunset.

Our first steps in Self-Directed Learning could have ended quite differently. The road closure could have been represented by a rigid view or belief on what, how, or when to learn. We could have turned back with tears, disappointment, and a feeling of failure, but instead, we chose the mindset of curiosity. We decided, as parents, to be more open to possibilities and creative ideas. Experimentation is about discovery. We can head into a new form of learning with a hypothesis of where we want to end up, but the process of getting there needs to be driven by curiosity. This sense of discovery has shown me how it develops creativity, interest, and adaptability.

The Process of Trial and Error

Experimentation also helps us to move through the process of learning. It opens up the opportunity to try and learn from our results by trial and error.

My son was always interested in being active and healthy. He was constantly seeking to challenge his physical abilities. When we started Self Directed Learning, his first instinct was to start surfing in the mornings. Since he didn't have to rush to school, he would wake up early, and we would drive him down to the beach to surf. This continued for around a year then, one day, he was curious about trying something different.

He experimented with skateboarding for a little while. He liked it, but the interest seemed to fade quite quickly. He spent more time re-visiting the idea. We talked about physical challenges, like daily push-ups or a boxing class. He tried but quickly became disinterested. This went on for almost a year. He was willing to try new things, but nothing would keep his attention.

This is the moment, as the parent, you start to feel that panic and lose trust. You know the one, right? The voice inside says, "He isn't going to stick with anything!" Or "He needs to learn how to be more disciplined."

We continued to talk about it, non-judgmentally, of course— this is the challenging part as a parent. We also need to practice curiosity and inquiry! He tried. He stopped. You could also see his confusion because he wanted to feel engaged and lit up by his choice but was still struggling to find the right solution.

We bought some weights for home, and he made a little mini gym in his room. He started lifting weights, making a workout plan, and then began enjoying the routine and this new path. He got to a level where he could no longer use the free weights and needed more. We got a squat bar and larger weights, and soon after, that wasn't enough. Within a year, he had developed a great routine and saw the results of his efforts. His mini gym was no longer enough to challenge him. We met a friend opening a gym in our area, so he was open to trying. That was it! The spark was ignited.

Years later, he continues going to the gym daily and has created multiple workout plans for himself and others. He has also completed his International Personal Training Certification and considers competing in Powerlifting.

I have seen in my son that the most successful, healthy, and active lifestyles come from doing things he enjoys. If you don't like team sports, try surfing, skateboarding, or the gym. He chose the gym. The same applies to learning. If you don't like Math, try Pattern Making or Chemistry. Find alternatives that work for you. It's about personalization over standardization. Find what lights you up and do more of that.

Experimenting with multiple ideas allowed my son to remain open to the process and try new things. He still surfs or skateboards for enjoyment with his friends but finds his weight training to fit perfectly for his lifestyle. Our conversations and his reflection helped him to acknowledge what he liked, didn't like, and what motivated him. He was continually adapting and developing his Sense of Self. He was witnessing the process of learning through trial and error.

A Stands for Action

> *"For the things we have to learn before we do them, we learn by doing them."*

> **- Aristotle.**

I can best describe action by sharing my learning journey in Public Speaking. To become a public speaker, I couldn't just read about it. I could study all I wanted, but it was a completely different feeling once I stepped onto the stage. Anyone that has done this can fully appreciate what I'm talking about! Speaking in public takes practice. I needed to experience it to truly understand. First, I needed to feel the fluttering in my gut, the sweaty palms, and the foggy terror. Then, I needed to dive into the experience to understand the intricate details, like eye contact, hand gestures, voice tonality, pausing, and stage movement. This is why action is necessary. It takes us deeper into the experience.

My son didn't learn about engines and motorbikes by reading about them. He took a motorbike apart at age 12. My daughter didn't know about prosthetics until she created a mold of her brother's toe. (This was so cool but a bit creepy.) My son didn't learn about potato guns by studying them, but he built one. My daughter didn't know about Special FX makeup by looking at pictures; she learned by creating hundreds of different looks.

At 11 years old, my daughter Khiana decided to commit to 100 Days of Makeup, which included imagining, creating, photographing, and posting to Instagram. Her feed included gruesome gore, blood, guts, and burns to hilarious illusions (like fingers as Churros covered in sugar and chocolate) and a full Sasquatch creation with hand-molded teeth and prosthetics. When she shared the results of her creativity, this led to more opportunities.

She got a weekly job at age eleven at a Local Family Event doing face painting. After almost a year of working at the event, they asked her to do a Special Effects Masterclass for kids. Because she showed up and took inspired action, she met new people at these events and ended up with more opportunities, doing makeup for photoshoots, birthday parties, school plays, and many Halloween parties. As her skills advanced, she required more advanced materials and dove deeper into the craft. She searched for a supplier and met the owner of a movie design studio in Bali, leading to more interest in film and set design. Her actionable steps in learning resulted in more opportunities. Her actions naturally guided her to the next steps.

Our children's knowledge came from engagement and inspired action, not passive learning. Jumping fully into projects and experimenting has led them to enjoy and be engaged with their education and to develop deeper, richer intricacies. It has helped them to learn about themselves and to see the next steps forward.

R stands for Reflection

This one was surprising and often struck me at the most unassuming times.

While we live in Bali, Indonesia (I'm originally from Canada), we went back to visit family. It was often strange for our kids because they would forget the cousins or friends they had met since the previous visit, which was often a year or more. A lot happens and changes in a year, so it often felt like they were meeting for the first time again. We would meet with a family, the adults would break off in discussion, and the kids would go to a playroom to hang out with the other kids.

One day, Khiana went off to play with the other kids, and later, we reflected on the time. She started by saying she was feeling quite shy. I paused and tried to understand. "What did you do? What did you notice?"

She paused and explained. "It wasn't a problem," she said. "I just became Philipo." As I mentioned earlier, Khiana was always creating detailed characters. Her favorite (and mine too) was Philipo. He was a bald, mustache-obsessed, taco-eating character, who juggled and sang his favorite song. So, she put on a bald cap and mustache and became him. He had his own Instagram account, a whole taco-loving family, and a suspenseful personal story.

"What did you notice?" I asked.

"Philip made everyone feel relaxed. The other kids instantly laughed and then wanted to play. It was easy."

Khiana learned that, with play and creativity, she was able to put others at ease, and they were able just to be themselves. Through more discussion, she learned that the characters she created were not only for her enjoyment but were tools for connecting with others. When we took the time to deepen our reflection, it resulted in rich and powerful learning.

When my son started surfing every morning when we began Self Directed Learning, my husband picked him up from the beach one day. He came home looking very pleased. "How did it go?" I asked.

"Good," he said.

"You catch some good waves?"

"Yup."

"Cool."

The next day, he had a meeting with his Learning Consultant, and I sat in the background to listen.

"What happened since our last call that you want to share?" she asked.

"I went surfing yesterday."

"Oh ya? How was it?"

"Good."

"Oh ya, why?"

Long pause.

"I caught some good waves."

"Oh ya. What happened?"

Another pause.

"Well, I was catching some waves, and it was good, but then this big wave came. I got excited and paddled hard. The timing was perfect. I was up on the wave, and it was like time stood still. The sun shone on my face, and the wind blew in my hair. I felt so in control and like I had all the time in the world."

I was nearly in tears. He had experienced this most miraculous feeling of flow, and I had washed over it with just a few casual words. I learned that day to ask good questions and then to wait (really wait) for the answer. I learned to stop filling in the blanks. That reflection time allowed him to acknowledge and integrate the experience into his consciousness. They discussed what it meant for him in his life and how he could bring more of that blissful feeling into his every day.

Developing the reflective muscle deepens learning and their sense of Self. They weren't rushing to get the desired result, like a test result or a finished presentation, but using each moment to observe and learn about themselves and others. When we took the time to deepen our reflection, it resulted in richer, more meaningful learning.

C stands for Change

As I mentioned, at the beginning of our Self-Directed Learning Journey, we moved from traditional schooling at home to unschooling towards a more Self-Directed Learning environment. At different steps along the way, our Learning Consultant (who has become an important part of our family today) would continue to ask us, "Is it working?"

This question, while it seems simple, genuinely shifted our thinking. Once we clarified and changed to meet our needs, we began personalizing our learning.

We started with hour-by-hour schedules at the beginning. "Is it working?" she would ask. The answer was a resounding NO. So, we continued to ask about subjects, work environments, and motivation and tried to find our own ways for it to work.

Another important part of Self-Directed Learning is Self-Evaluation. It is similar to reflection but helps us take steps forward or change how we navigate. Self-Evaluation is all about knowing how you actually feel and taking enough time to observe how you moved through the activity and what or how you want to change.

Was it exciting?

Frustrating?

Were you engaged?

Motivated?

What areas would you like to change?

How did you feel about the timing?

Was there enough time for exploration?

Were you able to sustain your energy throughout the project?

We had reached the end of a term and were doing a Self-Evaluation. The family gathered in the spare room with the Learning Consultant online, and the kids brought their slideshows and 'show and tell' items to include in their presentation. Colorful images and bold text flashed on the screen to summarize their projects. There was laughter, smiles, and frowns, all summing up the learning process. They shared what they had learned, and I felt proud of them and our family. I felt like we were finally getting into a stride. Finally, the kids had finished their presentations, and the Learning Consultant asked them, "Do you feel satisfied?"

They both took a quiet moment and answered, "No." I felt shocked and surprised!

This was another insightful moment for me, asking them if they felt satisfied or proud. I had never thought of doing that. My heart sank like I had been doing something wrong, or I hadn't fulfilled my role as the parent. I have now realized that this was not a reflection of me or us as a family, but rather that their accomplishments weren't in line with what was important to them. Khiana needed flow, balance, and creative expression. She valued family time together and doing the right thing. Java, on the other hand, valued seeing improvement and being enthusiastic. He needed to complete an exciting project but also feel challenged and able to see his self-improvement.

I witnessed the kids' willingness to adjust the course as they practiced more Self-Evaluation. The insight that I took away was the importance of clarifying what resulted, understanding how it made them feel, knowing what to change, and being okay to continue evolving.

H stands for Human Flourishing

While being happy may be the goal for our children in life, I prefer to think about the end goal as Human Flourishing, which is a broader sense of development based on the whole child. This could include physical and mental health, good close relationships, character, virtues and strengths, meaning or purpose, accomplishment, engagement or flow, and positive emotions like happiness.

What I have witnessed in our children during this Self-Directed Learning journey is a deeper and richer development of the whole person expressed in Human Flourishing.

It's about:

- having a sense of purpose because you have a choice,
- being engaged and motivated by curiosity and a willingness to take chances,
- taking inspired action,
- understanding yourself and having a profound capacity to accept others for who they are,
- reaching your potential while managing your physical and mental wellness,
- feeling good about your identity,
- feeling confident in the ability to navigate change,
- being connected with yourself and others,
- learning how to balance these different areas of life.

While, as humans, we are always searching for more, what I do think we need more of this.

More awareness

More experimentation

More inspired action

More listening

More choice

More focus on interests

More time and space

More reflection

More respect

More trust

More happiness

More human flourishing

When I think back to that afternoon with my husband on our leather couch, I realize what a pivotal moment it was. We were operating from a place of burnout. We'd both lost our sense of self and were desperately fighting to get it back. As a parent, I wanted to feel grounded in who I was, how I could function at my best, and give a solid example to our children of what human flourishing could look like.

This experience, personally navigating through it and witnessing it in our children, was exactly what I needed to find it in myself again, from understanding my body, health, and mind to knowing my strengths and abilities and honing in on my interests and desires. This is the gift I was given in this process.

I thank my children for walking with me on this journey, for being curious with me, and for allowing the world to emerge before our eyes as we took a step back to enjoy the process. This is what learning is all about.

 REMINDFUL *Life*

Resource

Below is a family values exercise that made a **huge difference in our family in the following ways.**

- We align with specific values based on our personal character, past, experiences, and a mixture of many elements. We each place importance on certain things.

- Understanding what each family member values and places importance on **helps us navigate our family life** and make decisions that work for our family and us as a whole.

- We had **important insights** and developed a deeper understanding of our family and how to function best as a family unit, while aligning with each other's values.

Remindful Life Family Values Reflection Tool

Talk with your family today and schedule some time to do this activity together. Print a copy of the charts below for each family member.

HINT: Make it fun & playful by creatively naming it or planning a special time together. Here's an example: Ice Cream Intermission - stop in the middle of the evening and bring out bowls of ice cream while you chat OR Mexican Family Fiesta - talk while you make tacos for dinner.

STEP 1: From the list, choose ten words or phrases that are important to you. Feel free to add other words or phrases in the space provided.

STEP 2: Think about what is <u>most</u> important to you. Circle your top three words.

MAIN WORD	DESCRIPTION
Accountability	Doing what you say you will do
Achievement	Reaching your goals
Balance	Balancing schoolwork and playtime
Commitment	Working hard on what we believe in
Compassion	Being kind and understanding
Competence	Being good at what you do
Continuous learning	Always learning
Cooperation	Working well with other people
Courage	Being brave
Creativity	Using your imagination
Enthusiasm	Being excited and confident
Efficiency	Making good use of time
Ethics	Doing the right thing
Excellence	Doing excellent work or sport
Fairness	Being fair
Family	Family

Financial stability	Having enough money
Friendships	Having friends
Future generations	Caring about the children of the future
Health	Keeping healthy
Honesty	Telling the truth
Humor/fun	Laughing and having fun
Independence	Able to do things on your own
Integrity	Being honest & trustworthy
Initiative	Making decisions for yourself
Making a difference	Making life better for others
Open communication	Talking openly & freely with others
Openness	Telling others about thoughts and feelings
Personal fulfillment	Having a full and happy life
Personal growth	Improving myself
Respect	Showing respect
Responsibility	Being responsible
Risk-taking	Being brave to try something new
Self-discipline	Controlling my behavior
Success	Being successful
Trust	Trusting others
Wisdom	Being wise

STEP 3: Complete the chart below.

Write down your three most import-ant values.	Why are these values important to you?	What do you do to show people these values? What are your behaviors?
1		
2		
3		

STEP 4: Set aside 30-45 minutes to share your worksheets with your family. Share stories about when you have seen them live their values. It's vital that you take the time to talk about it. Real learning occurs when you slow down and connect to listen with your heads and hearts.

STEP 5: Take a few minutes to write what you learned from this conversation in the chart below.

STEP 6: Even more fun: Plan a vacation based on these values.

This could be an actual vacation, the ultimate vacation, or just a pretend, imaginary vacation, whatever you choose.

Try to find ways that you could **respect and honor each other's values**. Listen closely to understand what others want to include in the vacation.

You can discuss or actually make an itinerary. You decide.

Make sure to take the time to **stop, reflect, and observe** yourself and your family during this activity. Some questions to ask yourself are these:

- What did you notice?
- What did you learn about yourself?
- What did you learn about others?

Use these playful, engaging activities to learn more about yourself and your family. Maybe you'll find something surprising or insightful in the process. We repeat this exercise every six months, but you can repeat this activity monthly or yearly and then adjust your decisions accordingly.

Above all, enjoy!

"Life is learning. **It's a balance between the heart and the mind."**

~ Khiana Kalli Gacek

CHAPTER NINE

Life Paint

By Khiana Kalli Gacek, Age 15

The blank canvas

Don't be afraid of a blank canvas.

I was a fourteen-year-old girl living in Bali with my family. My brother and I had already been self-directed learners for five years. Before that, I was at an international school but was searching for more time alone. I kept trying to fit it in, but at the end of the day, I felt exhausted. I had always needed time for reflection, and the constant busyness of school was just not for me.

Coming out of school, I stuck with the same friends. I hosted Halloween parties, went to sleepovers, and did anything a regular school kid would have done. As time went by, many of these friends left the island. The last standing were the closest. Finally, the last friend moved away forever, and I was left feeling helpless and alone.

I scrolled through Instagram, like any typical day, to see a mutual friend with a bunch of people, going out, seeing things, doing things, and going to parties. Each day, I waited patiently, checking my phone, wanting someone to reach out. I kept thinking to myself, "I'll just let fate handle it," as I painfully glared at the "no notifications" plastered on my lock screen. I sat there alone on my bed, waiting for some magical miracle, where I would be granted a big group of friends and unlimited invites until I realized that I could never meet new people if the furthest place I ever went was my kitchen.

I reached out to that mutual friend. Her life was filled with the fun and excitement that I was craving. I was chasing that teenage dream I saw in shows and movies. I sat anxiously as my stomach churned, waiting for a reply. Finally, she replied, wanting to meet up. I froze as soon as she stepped in the door, intimidated by her perfectly done makeup, fishnets, and tremendously big platform black boots that made it feel like she towered over me.

As she spoke, I noticed how different her life was to mine, fast-paced, impulsive, adventurous, rebellious! I was stunned. Everything felt so foreign yet intriguing. I felt like a blank canvas not yet painted by the world's experiences. I wanted to experience this lifestyle, but I knew I would need to adapt. I observed every new setting I was put in, subconsciously collecting data on the type of scenarios and people I'd be around. I became a chameleon. With this costume on, life didn't feel real. The decisions I made didn't matter much to me because I felt like I was never the one making them. I was mindlessly agreeing without having any real opinions. Life had no meaning. I was an empty vessel. I had become so distant from who I was and completely lost my sense of self. I felt like a robot being controlled by a mini-me inside. I started to wonder why.

Why did I want to change the person I was?

It started to remind me of how I felt when I was nine, my first existential crisis. Lovely. I used to lie on my brother's rooftop and stare blankly into the sky. It was a dome-shaped canvas of glistening stars and deep dark colors, but I was overwhelmed with those typical philosophical questions.

What am I working towards? What am I here for? Who am I, really?

I was never fully present because I was always floating through my own abyss of thoughts. To get myself through it, I pushed away these thoughts, along with my emotions.

The Scientist

Later that year, I started to notice a pattern, so I created a graph. It showed my ups and downs and advice for each stage. It helped a lot, especially when I hit the lows. Each stage had a name, beginning, the honeymoon phase, downfall, bottom, rock bottom, spike, plateau, dip, rise, and end.

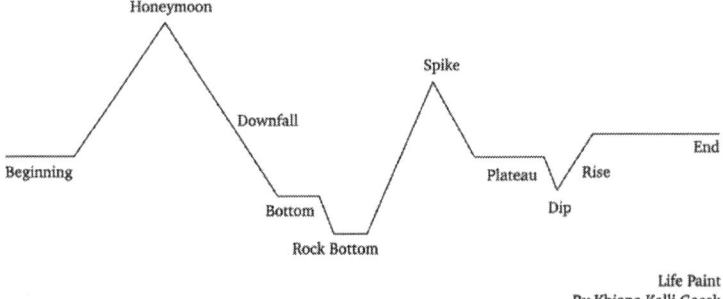

Life Paint
By Khiana Kalli Gacek

Before making the graph, I thought every upsetting moment would last forever. It felt like I was digging a deeper hole for myself that I struggled to get out of, but this time, I saw it all written on paper. I doubted its legitimacy at first until time passed and everything fit.

I was my own science experiment. I was doing a study on myself, collecting data, analyzing actions and thoughts, and always keeping track. Throughout that process, I learned a lot about myself and started to understand why I would do certain things or act a certain way. I went through life documenting each finding to create a well-rounded personal analysis until I found one fatal flaw.

I came across a big problem that challenged my research. I met a new friend, a guy. We spent a lot of time together. According to my research, he was perfect, but something was off. I spent hours ruminating over it, and my head overflowed with questions only I could answer. Every step I took to find an answer took me ten steps back again. It was a grueling cycle of confusion and uncertainty. Looking back, the answer was painfully obvious, but I was so blinded by my methods and rules that I didn't see that all I had to do was feel. It was a collision of my mind with my heart. I had to stop pushing emotions aside and face them head-on. I had to allow myself to feel.

My mind blew up into a million pieces. After all my contemplation, the answer was right in front of my face. Allowing myself to feel was the last piece in my puzzle of self. I didn't need to change who I was. Instead, I needed to understand and embrace my identity, which was there all along. Not only did I understand each stage of my graph, but I learned how to navigate my emotions within it.

Life Soup

Everything pieced together after what felt like a journey through hell and back. The graph was not only my science experiment of self but a tool for learning, living, and creating.

Over time, my world shifted. I had this newfound lust for life. The world felt vast, and the possibilities felt limitless. I fell in love with how the trees swayed, how the birds chirped, how the sun glistened, and how my dog got excited when he saw me.

I accepted each part of myself, along with my emotions. I began to see that the most beautiful art pieces throughout history were fueled by these feelings, transforming each empty canvas into a visual collage of intricate experiences. I dove further into art and music, embracing and celebrating my individual self-expression. I left doubt in the past and was free from toxic cycles. I felt my body was now a vessel for the person I'd always been. I continued to capture my self-expression and self-directed my projects in a way that honored who I was through fashion, art, and music.

I learned something more valuable than I would have ever imagined. *Life is learning.* It's a balance of the heart and the mind. The road of my learning journey isn't a straight highway but a bumpy, winding Bali road, where cows and chickens roam freely. And that's okay. Because I love chickens.

"As we change through one generation, we can raise a more conscious generation of children for the next."

~ Alisha Brache

CHAPTER TEN

Soul Aligned Education

By Alisha Braché

The New Paradigm of Children's Education has always appeared to me as a straightforward vision of inspirational change. From a young age, it has been something that I have been very passionate about. I have always known that I would not only be a witness to this shift in my lifetime but that I would be a part of it.

Why is that? Simply put, like all humans, when you experience a negative, traumatic, or misaligned experience, there is a deeper knowing within that the experience can and should be better. It sparks something in you. You can get angry or feel victimized by the situation or turn that anger into a fiery passion to do something positive. I am sure, in most cases, we go through both, and that is part of healing the human experience.

My life's work has evolved over the years. I have worked with all types of children, from the young ones suffering from tremendous trauma to the adults, still children in my eyes, who are suffering into adulthood because they were misunderstood by society.

By following my passion and intuition, I started my work full-time in 2017 under *Cosmic Gateway*, an education platform for adult children to help build awareness of energy sensitivity and to normalize the 'unseen world' so that people can help themselves through knowledge and information.

This led to the opening of *New Earth Children*'s social media platform in 2019, a platform designed to continue this work for sensitive children, Starseeds, parents, and caregivers.

I firmly believe the starting point in evolving general education and upbringing for children should be simple. Let's look at some basic categories:

Creative Expression:

Supporting creative expression is vitally important, as creativity is the life-giving energy we all possess. Yet, it often gets shut down early in modern society. Therefore, from a Soul or Energy perspective, disconnection from creative expression also disconnects us from our life-giving energy and inspiration.

When this occurs, it creates all sorts of problems, such as depression, anxiety, and a long list of potential "mental health" diagnoses. Unfortunately, this issue affects many in our world today.

I know there are many other compounding factors, including health, well-being, and environment. However, consider for one moment that the root cause of some people's depression or anxiety is the disconnection from their life-giving energy and creative inspiration. The remedy could be as simple as re-engaging in a creative endeavor that could spark them and 'cure' or 'heal' their "mental health" diagnosis. The fact we are seeing brilliantly effective remedies, such as Art and Sound Therapy, becoming more mainstream is a positive trend we can celebrate.

To have many different creative studies available for children, beyond what is currently offered, is crucial for this new paradigm of education. Things that could be included: sound healing, crystal bowls, creative writing, jewelry creation, creative exploration of food and cooking, architecture (for the more mechanically minded students), and innovative design opportunities.

A whole range of things that are *outside the box* could be possible, which will showcase that creative expression is for everyone, just in different ways! Below are some key areas that I believe can inspire new education methods.

Personal Self-Awareness:

Personal Self-Awareness is really about building and cultivating a good understanding of self. It is important for everyone, no matter their age, to know and understand themselves.

As adults, we spend lots of time trying to find out who we are. So often, we spend time and money on therapy, medications, and self-development, whether holistic or 'traditional.' This speaks to our disruptive contemporary society and how it often disconnects us from who we are at our core.

In most cases, when we journey to find ourselves, this is where the greatest change occurs and our most purposeful life and work begins. Now, imagine a learning environment that supports children's exploration of who they are, their unique gifts and talents, and what they are most passionate about. This would start their learning about themselves and set a framework to continue this exploration throughout their life. This would in turn promote positive self-awareness, confidence, and a sense of direction and purpose.

Self-awareness is also about developing each individual, looking at challenging behaviors and recurring patterns, and using personal self-awareness and strategies to establish positive and constructive behaviors. It can be a positive learning experience to see challenges, obstacles, learning difficulties, and growth opportunities. Furthermore, giving children support and tools to work with can be fun and motivating.

This is an overarching view of what an entire curriculum could be working towards: giving children a great chance to achieve more meaningful experiences and setting them up to pursue careers they are passionate about. People engaged in soul-aligned careers have the confidence, skills, and resilience to achieve wonderful, significant, fulfilling things.

We can also take a broader, society-wide view of what this kind of change might lead to. If everyone were immersed and grounded in these principles at an early age, it would forge a pathway to end many of the problems we see today, such as conflict, poverty, and injustice.

Life Skills:

This subcategory should be complementary to Personal Self-Awareness. Life Skills are something that I felt were very limited in the curriculum during my school years. However, they are critical for everyone to participate in society.

When I refer to Life Skills, I am not referring to looking for a job, resume writing, how to use money, banking, tax, etc., although I do think it is helpful to assist children to be able to go out and thrive in life and society in those areas. I am specifically referring to how to have good relationships, healthy boundaries, good conflict resolution and communication skills, and how to support your mental/emotional and physical well-being. Things like identifying when you're feeling hurt, unsupported, angry, and upset, and learning safe ways to express and understand your emotional needs.

These skills should be taught at home by our parents or caretakers; unfortunately, not all children have conscious and supportive parents, especially regarding these topics, because possibly the parents aren't even aware or know how to support themselves in this way.

If children had access to these tools, it would help them every day in every aspect of their life.

"As we change through one generation, we can raise a more conscious generation of children for the next."

Energy Awareness and safe places to explore intuitive abilities:

This is my personal favorite and what I am most passionate about! As a highly sensitive, intuitive, and psychic child, my struggles came in a different form than most children. Luckily, I had aware and supportive parents. However, I felt like the education system failed me, as I lacked confidence and didn't feel that I was good at anything because I didn't excel academically.

I found my confidence only came after leaving the education system. I found myself amongst spiritual groups, discovering teachers, mentors, and courses that helped me develop my intuitive, healing, and psychic abilities. I felt I belonged and was good at something for the first time in my life. But, of course, good is a bit understated; I excelled in these areas and pursued these things professionally as a young adult.

For all the sensitive, intuitive, energy healers and psychic children, especially those who are now adults who were not understood as children, life is very hard if you don't have supportive people and an understanding environment. This is what sparks my passion to help teach people about Energy Awareness, even before exploring intuitive abilities.

When you have these sensitivities, they are often misunderstood or misdiagnosed in unhelpful ways. Medication is prescribed, which only tends to make it worse or acts as a band-aid solution at best. Yet, if children who were interested and wanted to take an elective class were allowed to express their unique experiences and sensitivities freely and safely, talking about it can be healing and give answers. Children would have the opportunity to be taught how to utilize their abilities as 'superpowers' as intended, instead of regarding them as a disability.

Aspects of Energy Awareness can be taught, for instance, becoming aware of what your energy is compared to that of other people or how to empower your energy and keep it clear so that you're not empathically absorbing all the heaviness around you that can muddy your energy and make you feel depressed and lose your vitality. Once there is a baseline level of understanding around these things, teaching can progress into the more advanced studies of refining and utilizing gifts, like telepathy, psychic vision, remote viewing, and channeling energy, to help heal yourself and others. This would give an advantage to these rising stars in their own right because these are gifts and handy tools that can aid and help advance humanity's evolution.

I believe children are a gift to the world. I feel deeply that we can learn so much from them if they are given the safe space to show us how to be more connected to the unseen worlds, realms, and dimensions. This is just an aspect of all of us that most of us have forgotten, and they are here now to help us remember who we truly are and the gifts and abilities that we all have access to if we so desire.

The uniqueness of each child's soul:

From more of a spiritual and soul perspective, I believe that we all have a unique energy signature that comes from our soul's journey through various lifetimes.

Every experience we gain on a soul level stays connected with us in the form of energy, and we all have access to this, from the most incredible achievement and things we have mastered and crafted over many years/lifetimes to the most traumatic and horrifying events that leave us scared and fragile. All of this makes us who we are and sometimes can answer why we are how we are from birth, for example, personality traits and strong likes or dislikes for certain things.

For example, consider child prodigies who can play an instrument at a professional level without extensive training. This is a perfect example of a child tapping into their soul's abilities that were trained before this lifetime. Keeping in mind that we all have this on some level, the importance of being able to teach children by nurturing their uniqueness is vital to help these visible gifts flourish. It also helps support children with traumas or to overcome struggles that might not make sense in our conventional world.

When you apply energy and multidimensionality to these things, they provide *out-of-the-box* answers and creative ways to find solutions.

My future vision of education and the potential for humanity through the paradigm shift

For a long time, I have had a vision of a place where education takes place in a peaceful, fun, loving environment that is less clinical than it has been in the past.

It is a space that is a perfect balance of connection with the natural world and, at the same time, progressive and forward-thinking, which connects us to the stars and our cosmic origins beyond this world. It is a place where children can be supported in all their uniqueness to discover themselves and their particular traits as something to love and be proud of, where there is understanding for all and, above all else, the environment supports the individuals.

A New Paradigm of Education is where children can be all they are here to be and become in this world, where every child has the opportunity to express themselves fully, where they can utilize their gifts, abilities, intelligence, and soul wisdom to become good leaders, role models, parents, business owners, and teachers in the future. Each person has a positive contribution to society to make, a contribution that impacts the whole as one collective consciousness.

As a planet, we can heal, grow, and evolve, so that we can all meet our basic needs and get out of survival mode. We can feel empowered to walk boldly into the future and spend our time in fun and expansive ways to innovate and become a thriving civilization.

This may sound too idealistic for some, yet I know in my heart it is possible. I am not the only one. Many others have seen this vision, too, including the children. They know it is possible, as they are more connected with their hearts and souls and less bound up by the limitations of the mind.

I feel strongly there is a higher intelligence working through us that serves humanity's best interest. It brings everyone together at the perfect moment. That way, not only do individual projects around the world come together and collaborate, but the energy behind them is amplified. So, we can all move into a beautiful, brighter future with love, with *Soul Aligned Education* at the forefront of this beautiful New Earth we are all creating together.

Resource for Educators or Parents of Children/Teens:

Technique: Clearing your energy field.

Aim: Have energy awareness for the child and give them a tool/visualization technique to help support themselves if they are Empathic, Highly Sensitive, or having challenges with energy-related disturbances, such as lack of concentration, fears, sleeplessness, or behavior changes, such as mood swings and out of character behavior.

Timeframe: 10 - 30 minutes.

Set up before you begin: Set up a safe and comfortable environment that will be uninterrupted for the duration. Minimize, if possible, any loud noise, bright lights, or anything that could be overstimulating.

You can also include things to create a meditative environment, such as soft music, frequency sounds, soft lighting, pillows or blankets, and anything specific to the child/ren that will make them comfortable.

Instructions:

1. Before commencing:

    Ask the child/teen how they are feeling. Use open-ended questions to allow them the space to speak freely if they chose to do so. This can be helpful to create the intention (if so desired) for the process.

    You might want to use your own creative twist on this process to help facilitate something more specific to how they feel. For example, the child might be feeling anxious about going to school. You can get them to talk about where they handle the anxiety in the body, so they can have more body awareness of the feeling they are having. Then you can incorporate this information into this process.

2. Get your child to sit or lay comfortably. If they are likely to fall asleep, then get them to sit upright.

3. Start by guiding them through three deep breaths. If you wish, you can say that each inhale makes them feel more relaxed and allows them to let go of anything they think is necessary to release.

4. Continue this process for as long as needed, possibly longer than three breaths. Give them a few moments to find stillness.

5. Now, guide them with your voice to turn their focus inward and ask them to observe how their body and energy are feeling in this moment (you can let them reply aloud if you wish, but it's not strictly necessary).

6. Ask them questions to help the observation process.

   For example:

   Do you feel heavy or light?

   Do you feel calm or restless?

   Do you notice any parts of your body that feel uncomfortable?

7. Allow this part to be guided by their responses, or if they aren't communicating, use your intuition to lead this process, allowing a depth of awareness around their present energy state.

8. When they are ready to move on to the next phase, invite them to call in a color of light.

For example:

This could be like a shower of light streaming down from the top of their head to wash over their entire body, or it could look different. It can vary with each individual. Allow them to choose the color that comes to them, as this always has significance to their unique energy signature (individuality is important.)

9. You might give the child/ren tips to guide this energy color to specific parts of their body. For example, if they have identified anxiety in their stomach, it can go there to help soothe that area.

10. When you're finished working with the color of light, ask them to visualize grounding that energy color and their feet into the ground to help bring them back to a more grounded state of awareness.

11. Start to guide them back, allowing them to take another three deep breaths, with each breath bringing more awareness back into the body, back into the room, and back into the now.

12. After they have come back and opened their eyes, you can ask them questions about how they are feeling now as opposed to before the process. Then, if they have found it helpful, discuss how they could use the process at other times to help support themselves.

"As we cross the bridge to a more awake and loving world, we will change on many levels; raising changemakers together."

~ Heidi Conway

CHAPTER ELEVEN

Educating our Young People – Together We Rise *'The Changemaker Way'*

By Heidi Conway, Coach and Edupreneur

"My daughter was suicidal and in hospital. She had a traumatic high school experience and had decided that life was not worth living. I didn't know how to save my daughter, and all the expert mental health professionals were struggling. Just when I was about to give up any hope left, her idea of saving the turtles in Costa Rica appeared. During one of our intense conversations, my daughter told me that she was worried about the endangered sea turtles. The communication we had about saving the turtles would save my daughter's life. By becoming a changemaker and an advocate for a purpose far greater than her own personal trauma, she healed herself...

This is the Changemaker Way." - Linda Johnstone, Co-Author of *The Changemaker Way*

"I have two sons. The eldest son was diagnosed neurodiverse at age seven, and by the time he was a tween, he struggled with

*change and expressing himself in written form. His teacher told
me he refused to write, yet in the first week of homeschooling,
we realized he just was not writing in the timeframe the teacher
wanted him to, plus he wanted to draw the characters and
scenery first, and then write about it. My younger son's teacher
said that he was not focusing, and we discovered that, like the
eldest, we didn't need to worry that he wouldn't be prepared for
his future. He could focus, just not on the curriculum content or
the way it was taught in the classroom. What was only meant
to be for seven months of building confidence, resilience, and
willingness to learn transformed into certainty that education
is to be enjoyed using the purpose-based approach, similar to
what I had used to coach adults since 2001.)...*

This is the Changemaker Way." - Heidi Conway, Co-Author
of *The Changemaker Way*

I have been a life coach since 2001, helping adults transform
their lives. It wasn't until I had children that I realized how
much traditional education holds adults back from fulfilling
their true potential. Schooling is focused on preparing adults
for the daily grind of 9-5 employment, for entering a world
of competition, unhealthy reward triggers, and material
accumulation. It's no wonder adults struggle to find meaning
in their lives after they have spent the first 15-20 years of it in
a system designed to pump out sameness.

After the birth of my own children, and their personal
struggles with change, writing, and focus, I joined the home
education movement, absorbing as much as I could from
listening and watching how they learned and also from talking
with other mothers who had been home educating for years.

I soon realized that the purpose of home education was not for me to become a substitute traditional teacher within the comfort of my lounge room and kitchen. My role was to educate my children in an entirely different way to the mainstream school system; we embarked on real learning.

That's how I became a Changemaker Coach for my own children and for hundreds of others. I have created a new paradigm for educating teens, which focusses parent educators on being the change they want to see in the world, actively listening to their children with their head and their hearts and learning to communicate confidently with love (not fear) so that there is enough space for the young people in their lives to grow and change.

Coaching your young person opens opportunities for personal parental transformation, too. Homeschooling, focused on nurturing changemaker teens, taught me about self-reliance and how to embrace, navigate, and create authentic learning experiences for both my children and myself.

It also raised the frequency of my own 'being.'

I am a product of traditional schooling, too. My own school experiences included mainly learning what my parents thought imperative for me to learn and them often finishing my projects for me, because I either didn't enjoy the work and they didn't want me to fail or not having enough time due to all the extracurricular classes I attended. As I entered adult life, I took with me those flawed teachings, resulting in a series of life events, a personal Armageddon that included divorce, job loss, bankruptcy, a major car accident, and an eating disorder. Like so many adult women, on top of my own challenges, I was also caring for people with various challenges in their abilities, my son, who is neuro-diverse, and a close relative who suffered from dementia.

In coaching my teens beyond the classroom, I was also able to make changes to my own life, walking away from everything that kept me stuck in the old way of learning and disconnected from my soul.

I was able to be vulnerable and reconnect to myself, discovering my passion and original purpose of showing people the magnificence within them. Through my coaching, speaking, and facilitating, I realized I am able to help clients create a healthy and meaningful life and be financially rewarded for the work they enjoy. I realized that, not only could I help my young people learn from home, but I could earn from home, too. I walked away from my six-figure corporate job income in health, safety, and environmental management, choosing instead to focus on coaching teens and adults, starting with my own boys and a small group of adult clients.

Transitioning professionally in this way became a real-life example for my children. They saw the changes I was prepared to make to achieve a connection to my dreams and began re-connecting to themselves and their soul desires. They gained confidence and learned to voice who they were, following a self-directed learning path rather than squeezing themselves into a templated model of success defined by traditional schooling.

They uncovered and discovered more deeply their own way of being themselves, their Changemaker within.

What is the Changemaker Way?

The Changemaker Way™ is a meticulously designed facilitated online coaching system to help young people let go of contention and fear of separation to instead discover a profound connection to themselves, their learning, and the appropriate curriculum. This connection allowed them to pursue their passion and purpose and be confident, happy, and positively future-ready. The connection between us grew as well, as we lived skills needed for the changing world of empathy, curiosity, and vulnerability. The more I could see evidence my teenagers were thriving naturally and clearly on purpose, the more my sleepless nights of worry diminished. I now have certainty I did, and am still doing, the right thing with regards to teenagers' education.

From the struggle or emotional contention with themselves, the possible lack of time and attention available by caregivers, with anxiety from past traditional educational environments and experiences, or for other reasons, young people aged twelve to twenty-five often begin their way on the changemaker journey being shy, lost, anxious, bored, apathetic, confused, or doubting their ability to learn. Some teens reject or are deceptive when it comes to work on offer, yet it is very soon clear they all have a certain goal that is important to them to be fulfilled.

We assist students experiencing challenging emotions and deficits in communication, social and life skills to develop skills to integrate confidently as a focused and contributing adult in the community. For this reason, we support mothers and mentors of young people to identify appropriate social learning environments, for their young person to connect confidently with themselves and be clear on the way forward as they work in a structured, yet flexible way. Learning occurs when environments are physically, emotionally (mental health), and identity safe, allowing the teen to be themselves unconditionally.

Changemaker Teens – How we coach young people

The Changemaker Way has four modules for young people to complete. The first three are covered over eight sessions with their personal coach.

Module One focuses on self-discovery and exploration. It poses questions to the young person that promotes both imagination and critical thinking. The young person's passions for learning are clarified, and a unique one and five-year vision for a meaningful life is created. For older youth, a ten-year vision is also developed. There is a high potential for this step to uncover and confirm a long-term vocation or career.

Module Two encourages the young person to express their Hero's Journey verbally via illustration or song, or by writing a story, play, or poem.

Module Three encourages and allows the youth to design and take initiative for the 'how' of their own learning and record it in a comprehensive and individualized learning plan. This is the module where self-directed, self-motivation, and self-organization goals are scaffolded and embraced with ease. The action plan is in the ideal format with the flexibility to be tailored for both neurodiverse and neurotypical learners. Lifeskills are made clear, fun, and successfully implemented.

This learning journey is mapped and used to determine career paths, including entrepreneurial endeavors, future study, and any additional support and experience required.

Module Four identifies how The Changemaker Way of learning can influence the family as well as the local and global community. The individual learning plan is prepared to be presented as a project for sharing.

The program allows young people to become crystal clear on what they would like and how to get it whilst learning the recognized curriculum components in an inspiring, safe, practicable, and life skill-enhancing way. Parents are invited to attend the last session to see first-hand what their young person has discovered and how they can support them with learning environments and resources moving forward.

Changemaker Parents – How we coach parents to coach their teens

The Changemaker Way envisages the parent not as a teacher but as a life coach and facilitator. Supporting a teen requires the parent (usually the mother), to hold the space for transformation, which is one of the skills taught in the content in the specific training, 'A Course for Raising Changemakers™' that with The Changemaker Way completes The Raising Changemakers Mastermind™, which is becoming rapidly known and being experienced as a thought and communication system based on love rather than fear.

Each learner requires a very specific educational plan that supports 21st-century skills that prepare for life-long learning, career direction, and joyful life. Experience with implementation of the integrated supports detailed below are with young people aged 12-25 and have shown effective and beneficial results of:

- Increased and clear direction.

- Confidence to engage in meaningful activities and conversations,

- Self-esteem to have the willingness to set and achieve goals, and

- Maturity to begin building meaningful relationships.

- Knowing and creating a sense of safety in peer groups to allow appropriate interaction, which has led to successful entry into further studies in higher education, for example, College and University, with support from as early as age 15.

Parents are taught to use coaching skills and step-by-step techniques to support the learner to close the gap between dependent learning and to increase student confidence in becoming a happy, confident, fulfilled, and contributing member of society.

The steps to achieve these outcomes focus on five main priority goals:

- Independent learning

- Self-directed learning and living (life skills)

- Self-motivated

- Self-organized

- Self-directed career

We believe it is vital to involve the primary caregiver in this process so the student can practice at home what they learn during their sessions with our facilitators, coaches, and tutors. Mothers and mentors model changes required in their own lives in appropriate and significant ways, reducing the stress and overwhelm and instead bringing increasing ease and understanding to the relationship with the learner and the family each step of the way.

What success looks like for Changemaker families

The Changemaker Way supports young people and their families with alternative learning by way of a self-directed life. It allows families to create the physical and emotional space for their children to discover, create, and clearly see the vision of their true self. The learning occurs in a way that ensures an exciting future of meaning, passion, and purpose, taking intelligent, deliberate, and conscious action to become real changemakers.

Changemaker families shift the trajectory of their lives, moving away from the stress of learning to fit into the world, which often leads to pain when we can't mould ourselves to unrealistic expectations, and allowing everyone to do what they were born to do.

The whole shift when experiencing the 'Raising Changemakers Pathway' comprising 'A Course in Raising Changemakers' and 'The Changemaker Way,' whether as an adult or young person, respectively, is to give birth to your true self lovingly with ease, with love and not fear. The unconscious focus is no longer on the separation of birthing, but instead, it's all about the connection. By learning about the authentic self,

Changemaker families bring their skills and gifts to the planet. They heal themselves, and they heal the world.

This is a fundamental rise of wisdom and shift in the education paradigm.

Instead of educating young people to be adults of apathy (and experiencing the pain of disconnection whether that is mental health issues, suicide, family breakdown, school shooting or global war and catastrophe), searching their whole lives for connection to themselves, The Changemaker Way promotes life-long learning in pursuit of all that we love to do and be. In turn, that love changes the world.

Changemaking is an opportunity to bring alignment to soul, genius, passion, and purpose. When we do this, we transcend industrialized learning and allow ourselves to shine and thrive. As a result, families have more freedom and spiritual independence.

"The most regretful people on earth are those who felt the call to creative work, felt their own creative power restive and uprising, and gave to it neither power nor time."

- Mary Oliver

Raising Changemakers by coaching a teen (or a parent) in The Changemaker Way is definitive but gentle.

Yet, its impact is profound.

Greater self-love, awareness, and healing consciousness open up even greater possibilities for the entire world. When we all deal with the pain of traditional schooling and work, a collective pain diminishes and is reframed. We transition from fear to love.

At times, I have felt judged by people for seeking joy and love ahead of all else. I have been warned away from creating unrealistic expectations for parents, educators, and young people.

Being a Changemaker means embracing possibility, vulnerability, and optimism. It does not mean being perfect or self-absorbed or inflexibly focused on outcomes. Being a Changemaker can be very messy, as you encounter contrast and resistance to change and practice transformative ways of being.

The world is relying on individuals and families to make a change and transform. The climate needs change: a world of pandemics and illness needs change; a world of war needs change. Awareness is rising. Education is becoming real. A Changemaker coach can hold the space for you in the messy moments and guide you on doing the same for yourself and those you adore.

Individually, as a family, as a community, as a society, as the inhabitants of a glorious world, we ache for a beautiful and meaningful life. One of the first questions we are asked as children is, "What do you want to be when you grow up?"

The answer does not lie in an aspirational career or an ideal level of wealth. The answer is always happiness and love. I breathe and continue to walk my talk. I focus on my own inspired evolution and on Linda's and my vision of being the Changemaker we are all born to be as we live a meaningful life by sharing what we learn with sincere appreciation.

VERSE 1
GIVE ME YOUR HAND
AND I'LL GIVE YOU MINE
OPEN UP YOUR HEART
BODY SOUL AND MIND

VERSE 2
BREATHE AND FEEL
EMOTIONS SO REAL
SURRENDER TO TIME
LET THE UNIVERSE ALIGN

PRE-CHORUS
THIS IS JUST THE BEGINNING
SO TRUST IN YOURSELF
AND LET LOVE IN
REACH INSIDE AND YOU WILL FIND
THE TRUTH IS THERE IN YOUR OWN EYES

CHORUS
LOVE IS THE KEY
TO SET US FREE
THE LIGHT IN YOU
IS THE LIGHT IN ME

VERSE 3
EVERYONE HAS NEEDS IN THIS WORLD
EVERYBODY JUST WANTS TO BE HEARD

VERSE 4
BREATHE AND FEEL
EMOTIONS SO REAL
REMEMBER WE'RE PART
OF THE ONE HUMAN RACE
BUT WE ALL MOVE
AT OUR OWN PACE

PRE-CHORUS
SO PUT ONE FOOT IN FRONT OF THE OTHER
MOTHER, FATHER, SISTER AND BROTHER
BE THE CHANCE THAT WE WANT TO SEE
WE CAN UNLOCK THOSE CHAINS
YOU AND ME

CHORUS
LOVE IS THE KEY TO SET US FREE
THE LIGHT IN YOU IS THE LIGHT IN ME
WITH A LITTLE FAITH
WITH LOVE AND GRACE,
WHAT A DIFFERENCE WE CAN MAKE
LOVE IS THE KEY TO SET US FREE
LOVE IS THE KEY

BRIDGE
LISTEN TO YOUR SOUL
AND IT WILL FLOW LIKE A RIVER
LISTEN TO YOUR HEART
AND IT WILL GUIDE YOU
LAY DOWN YOUR ARMS AND BE STILL
WHEN YOU KNOW COMPLETE SURRENDER
THE UNIVERSE WILL DELIVER

CHORUS
LOVE IS THE KEY TO SET US FREE...

RAISING
Changem*ker*Teens

© GARRY SMITH 90% HEIDI CONWAY 10%

206

"We need to shift our perception of who children are and our relationships to them; our role in their lives. Children don't belong to us. They are not 'ours.' If we're lucky, for a short period in time, we have the privilege of supporting, protecting, and nurturing them."

~ Sian Goodspeed

CHAPTER TWELVE

The Dawning of a New Paradigm

By Sian Goodspeed

If you are reading these words, you're probably already aware of some of the problems within the education system and are likely wondering what we can do to bring about change.

This is not a new dilemma. For decades, educationalists and well-known figures have been calling for a different approach to education, as have many teachers and parents. Yet, very little has changed, and the old paradigm has persisted...until now.

The past few years have brought great upheaval to schools and educational institutions worldwide. Whilst this has been devastating in many ways, it's also created a unique opportunity for galvanizing a shift toward a *new* educational paradigm. Enforced lockdowns and the switch to temporary homeschooling gave parents from all walks of life a unique insight into what and how their children were being taught in school. The experience has left many questioning why we persist with the same outdated educational approaches that are not serving many of our children.

These are questions I've been ruminating over for some time: Why do we restrict our children to learning about specific things, all at the same time, whether or not they are interested in the subject matter? Why do we compare, measure, and test them as though they should all aspire to the same goals? What is the point? Why are we wasting their talents, creativity, and uniqueness?

Over my lifetime, I've experienced the English education system from many angles. In fact, as a parent, teacher, and owner of a tuition business, I've spent much of my adulthood supporting the old school-based educational paradigm in some way or another. It may therefore come as a surprise to read that my 'big vision' for a New Paradigm of Education doesn't involve schools at all!

Before I elaborate on my vision, I'd like to explain how I arrived at such unconventional views and, to put my ideas into context, I'm going to outline my own educational experience.

My educational journey

My personal experience of the education system started many decades ago when, aged five, I joined a small primary school in England. I enjoyed learning and progressed fairly uneventfully through those years, moving up to secondary school at eleven. Unfortunately, at that point, my educational experience began to go downhill.

Looking back, I later realized that, although I was at a 'good' school, it wasn't the right fit for me. My former interest in learning and my quiet self-confidence plummeted as I was subjected to a seemingly relentless focus on working hard, homework, tests, and exams. By the time I left, aged eighteen and with three disappointing A-Level grades in subjects in which I had no particular interest, I'd lost all motivation for learning. What's worse, over my time at secondary school, I'd concluded I was stupid, developed low self-esteem, and lost my passion for the things I'd previously loved to do.

Of course, I can only speculate as to whether the outcome would have been better had I attended a different school. However, I suspect that, although my day-to-day experiences would have differed to some degree, the dents in my self-confidence and self-esteem were the consequence of the educational paradigm in which it was entrenched rather than a direct fault of the school itself.

Following on from school, I took a gap year before moving on to university, where I rekindled some of my former love of learning and self-confidence, and I discovered that I wasn't perhaps as stupid as I'd thought. Studying subjects that interested me and having more choices over study methods and assignments meant I performed better than I ever had at school. I still found exams intimidating but managed to get through them by taking Bach's 'Rescue Remedy' to calm my nerves and memorizing essay outlines that I could regurgitate in the exam hall.

During my final year of university, I decided to pursue a teaching career. Looking back at my school years, I realized my academic challenges were not due to a lack of ability but the result of my emotional state and eroded self-belief. I could see these were consequences of the learning environment and teaching approach, rather than something intrinsically 'wrong' with me. I wanted to help students to have a more positive learning experience than I had, so I enrolled in a teacher training course and, in 1996, I began my first year as a primary school teacher.

Over the following years, I taught across the primary age range (five to eleven years old) in a mix of state and private schools. Throughout it all, I aimed to prioritize my students' emotional well-being, creating a learning environment that fostered teamwork, trust, and support. My classroom management style stemmed from an early training in assertive discipline during my first teaching post, focusing on mutually agreed rules and students taking responsibility for their behavior. 'Good choices' were rewarded with stickers, class points, and certificates, whereas 'poor choices' led to consistent, proportionate consequences.

In 2008, after twelve years in the primary classroom, I left school life behind to set up my education business, Flying Start Tuition. Not long after, I encountered neuro-linguistic programming (NLP) and subsequently trained as an NLP practitioner. During that weeklong training, I remember thinking: *If only I'd known all this when I was a schoolteacher. Even better, had I known it when I was a student!*

Following on from my practitioner course, I embedded NLP techniques into the teaching and learning programs at Flying Start. These techniques help our students to learn more effectively, grow in confidence, and handle emotional states such as anxiety and stress. NLP continues to form part of our holistic approach to education, an approach that values well-being and mindset, alongside skills and knowledge.

This decision shaped how the business has evolved and was the beginning of my disentanglement from the belief systems embedded in the old educational paradigm. My NLP training was life-changing, not only in its impact on my business (and the students who have passed through its doors), but also in how it transformed my understanding of human behavior and how I see myself, others, and the world in general.

A shift in my perspective

When my eldest daughter, Charlotte, was six, we decided to remove her from school to educate her at home. Her younger sister, Ava, was home-educated from the outset. Our journey into home education opened my eyes to possibilities other than school-based learning. Through this process, I understood far more about how children (and adults) learn than I had as a teacher. However, my shift away from the mindset of the old paradigm didn't happen straightaway.

Whilst my approach to education was quite progressive in many ways, it was based upon the old paradigm 'comply and achieve' ways of thinking. Back then, I bought into the commonly held assumptions that a good education meant achieving good grades (whether at home or school) and that children needed to do what the teacher (or, in my case, their mother) asked them to do.

This attitude was ingrained in me. Throughout my teaching career, I had run my classrooms on the foundations of collective decision-making and positive rewards rather than criticizing, blaming, or punishing, but the underlying assumptions were the same: students should be obedient, hard-working, and (for the most part) attentive. So, even though I may have rejected some elements of the existing paradigm, I didn't question the foundations upon which the paradigm was built.

Given my teaching background, it is hardly surprising that, when we first embarked on our homeschooling path, I envisioned our approach would be mainly school-at-home, interspersed with home education tutor groups and educational outings. However, as my ideas about education began to loosen up, the 'school at the home' part was dropped relatively early, and over the years, we shifted to a more free-flowing, autonomous approach often referred to in-home educating communities as 'unschooling.'

Alongside my experiences in the home education world, my NLP Practitioner course rekindled a thirst for learning that was the catalyst for my ongoing program of self-development that, a few years later, led me to non-violent communication (NVC).

I'll be honest, when I first sought out NVC training around 2014, my motive was still entrenched in the old paradigm – my aim being to get my children to comply in the nicest way and with the least resistance possible! As my training progressed and my understanding deepened, I came to realize that this is not the point of non-violent communication at all! Whether communicating with a child or another adult, the underlying principle is acceptance and connection, rather than being a *nice* way to persuade others to do what you want. This realization transformed how I communicate with myself and those around me, and it also triggered some fundamental shifts in how I view parenting and education.

The shaping of a vision

My ongoing personal development, through training, reading, and research, together with my experiences as an educator and parent, have combined to shape my vision of a new educational paradigm. Alongside the emergence of this vision has been my growing awareness of the systemic influences that created and still perpetuate the old paradigm.

I now believe that we come into this world with all the wisdom and resources we need to unlock our purpose and potential. Children are born free of judgment and self-doubt and full of trust, wonder, and awe. From the moment we're born, we start to learn. Learning is what we do all the time. It's a natural, intrinsic part of being human.

For many, school takes away our natural sense of curiosity, the ability to learn for the joy of learning, to find out things for ourselves. Instead, it teaches us to look to others for approval, to trust others to tell us what to do, what to learn, what's right and what's wrong, to judge whether we are failures or successes, to decide if we are good or bad.

Don't get me wrong, there are many amazing schools and many more wonderful teachers. I fully believe that most teachers have the best intentions for their students. They work long hours and are committed to making school a positive experience. I certainly don't doubt that teachers can and do make a powerful impact on many children. But the system is fundamentally flawed, and most of them are unwittingly reinforcing it.

If you think about it, most of what children are taught in schools is for the sole purpose of demonstrating that children can pass an exam. We spend years trying to cram irrelevant facts into the minds of our children. Facts they will mostly have forgotten a few days after they've been taught them, facts they can now find at the tap of a button in the moment they actually need them...if they ever do. Yet so many skills that are vital for humans to thrive, to *survive*, are not even on the school curriculum.

Children don't need to be crammed full of facts. They don't need to be told who to be or what to aim for. Given the proper support and a nurturing environment, children *will* learn. They just need to be given the space, freedom, and loving support to explore this for themselves.

In fact, children often learn best with a hands-off approach. I know from my own experience that children can and do learn without being explicitly taught, and there are countless other parents, educators, and researchers who know the same.

Take reading, for example many children learn to read without any formal instruction. Although both my daughters had some initial instruction, when they were left to their own devices and given the freedom to choose what to read (rather than school reading scheme books,) their reading took off.

What's more, many children who are taught *fail to learn*. Anyone who has worked in education will know that many children struggle at school and need extra support, but to what extent are their struggles a direct consequence of trying to fit the child into the system, rather than allowing the system to be shaped by the child? How many children are being taught subjects that don't interest them, using methods that don't work for them, in an environment that is not suited to them? What is the real impact of this dogged approach to education?

It is certainly not a new revelation that the one-size-fits-all approach to schooling doesn't serve many of our children. It is fairly common for children to be deemed as having gaps in their learning and to require extra support in order to 'catch up' with their peers. These gaps only exist because of the old paradigm values in which the schools are entrenched, the idea that all children *should* meet certain standards at a certain age and in a certain way. How about, rather than asking where the children 'should' be and how to 'fix' them, we ask if the existing educational paradigm is actually creating these problems in the first place? [9]

A school system based upon testing and measuring is, by design, labelling many children as 'failures' from an early age. In so doing, it's teaching them that they're not good enough, they need to try harder, and they must do more. Yet, how many children have other strengths and talents that are unseen because they are locked into a system that values a narrow range of academic subjects over everything else?

The sad consequence of this approach is that our children learn not to follow their passions, nor to harness their inner guidance but to self-judge, self-criticize, and doubt themselves. They are raised not to think critically, not to form their own opinions, nor to express themselves truthfully, but to follow the crowd. Over time, these once wise, bright-eyed, eager beings, full of awe and wonder, grow into adults who are disillusioned, dissatisfied, depressed...disconnected.

Disconnection is the root of all problems

In fact, I believe that disconnection causes many of the problems we see in the world today. Disconnection within: between our mind, body, heart, and soul. Disconnection

---

9   For more thoughts on this, please see: Clements, Je'Anna, *What if Schools Create DYSlexia?*

from each other. Disconnection from Nature. Disconnection from life. Disconnection from our divinity. Because we are disconnected, we lose our sense of purpose, joy, and ability to love ourselves, and others, unconditionally.

We are driven by the urge to meet our needs by any means possible, based upon the assumption that resources are limited, and we need to compete to get them. And because we are taught to compete, we judge ourselves and often find ourselves lacking. We judge others in the same harsh, unrealistic way too. This reinforces our separation, leading to criticism, blame, anger, and conflict.

This way of thinking and behaving is deeply embedded in our psyches by the conditioning we receive from birth, through our cellular memory, from our memories of past lives, and the individual and collective traumas we've experienced throughout history.

Education in our modern western world is designed to mold children into model citizens of a framework based upon the presuppositions of scarcity, competition, and right/wrong thinking. This is the 'winners and losers' version of living. It's a model that teaches our children they must work hard to compete for the world's limited resources.

A 'good education' is regarded by many as essential for children to have the best chances of being successful and functioning well as adults in society. Yet, so many adults are not functioning well at all. In fact, many adults go through life in a daze – constantly busy, frazzled, stressed out, and living for a couple of days off each week.

Sadly, many of our children are not functioning well either. It's clear from the statistics that children's mental and physical health problems are on the rise. Whether or not it's the sole cause, this work-hard, competitive approach to life is certainly not helping.

Hence, the existing educational paradigm is not the problem. It's part of a much bigger problem, a symptom of the mechanistic, disconnected way of living that has become predominant in our modern western culture.

Therefore, to move toward a new paradigm of education, I believe we need to change how we think about life and living. We need a collective shift from disconnection to connection.

A connected approach

I believe that connection, within ourselves and with others, is essential to move us away from a divided world, full of inner and outer conflict, towards a more harmonious, peaceful, and sustainable way of being. We connect with ourselves by nurturing our heart, body, mind, and spirit, by discovering what brings us joy and by following our passions. We connect with others by letting go of judgment and blame, by fostering empathy and exercising compassion.

Crucially, we need to understand how we are all connected and part of Nature – that the world is an interconnected whole. If we can reconnect with, nurture, and heal Nature, we will also be nurturing and healing ourselves. From this place of connection, we will achieve balance, harmony, and joy.

It's clear that, rather than helping us to foster these connections, the prevailing paradigm of education (and living) serves to divide us.

My vision of a new paradigm of education

So, you may now understand why my 'big vision' is a world without schools - at least not in the sense of institutions where parents send their children for much of the week. (I don't believe the separation of children from their families for large chunks of their childhood is necessary or desirable.)

Instead, I envision community-based living and learning, where people live together harmoniously and interdependently, where skills are shared, and resources are allocated according to need.

Where there are no deadlines, no 'must dos,' 'should haves,' no judging and blaming. Instead, we would live with acceptance and connection, living joyfully and freely, nurturing ourselves and our children, and taking responsibility for our health and wellbeing.

In this new paradigm, there are no labels; no one is 'better' than anyone else. Instead, we are all accepted as we are, as unique individuals with our own, unique way of perceiving the world and our exceptional skills, talents, challenges, and needs.

My vision in this new paradigm is learning *through* life. Education *is* life, and life *is* education. There is no need for a distinction between the two. I believe we are innately designed to learn what we need to learn, when we need to learn it, and that having this freedom to learn is a fundamental feature of the new paradigm. This freedom will enable our children to explore their unique talents and gifts, follow their passions, and shine.

Education in this new paradigm may come in many forms. I love the idea of community-based learning hubs for all ages, where adults and children learn together, following their passions and sharing their skills and knowledge.

I'm not envisioning returning to the nomadic, tribal, tech-free ways of old (although if that is what calls to you, then go for it!) In fact, I am not envisioning any one specific model. Different forms of living will appeal to different people, and I believe that, given the freedom to choose, people will naturally gravitate toward the path that calls them.

This is not just a new way of educating. It's a new way of living. Of being. More than that, I believe it's the next stage in human evolution – a crucial stage if we are to avert global disaster and avoid mass extinction.

It won't happen overnight, and it won't come from the policymakers, the governments, or the world powers. Those people are so entrenched in the old paradigms. They have little or no incentive to change.

What can we do within the existing system to move toward the vision?

While my longer-term vision is for a completely new way of living and educating, I am painfully aware that these changes will take time – generations. I believe there are plenty of steps we can take now, as educators and parents, to start the shift towards a more connected approach.

Many shifts are already taking place around us as increasing numbers of parents are calling for change within the existing education systems, many of whom are looking for alternatives to mainstream schools. Notably, the home education community has been growing steadily and has seen a sharp influx over the past few years.

It's heartening to see many parents and educators coming together to create alternative learning hubs for children. This is a promising sign and one that I welcome. However, I hope that, rather than finding new ways to deliver the same knowledge-based, exam-driven curricula, people will think outside the box and look at the bigger picture.

It's clear that we need urgent solutions to the world's problems, and our young people need the freedom to be imaginative, creative, and inventive so they can come up with those solutions. To avert global crises and repair the damage that has been done, we need to equip our children with the skills to collaborate, communicate, and thrive. We need to be fostering the brilliance of our young people now – not wasting their formative years teaching them irrelevant skills and filling them with redundant knowledge.

To be clear, I'm not calling for a ban on all academic subjects. Some children have a passion for mathematics or science or English. However, I would like to see a much more rounded, balanced education available to all children, an education incorporating life skills, emotional and social intelligence, spirituality, creativity, imagination, deeply embedded with nature, and community involvement.

I'd also like to see much greater flexibility within the current education system to allow children the freedom of self-directed learning. Rather than teaching pre-determined content, I would like to see children being taught how to learn effectively and encouraged to follow their interests and passions, with educators acting as facilitators rather than dictators.

I would also love to see flexi-schooling being a real option for families who would like to go down that route. (This is something we tried for a year with our daughter, and she loved it, but sadly the school wouldn't allow her to continue for more than a year.) I believe this could be beneficial to schools, too, enabling smaller class sizes and easier allocation of resources each day.

Around the world, there are many examples of different educational models, including democratic and Steiner schools, that I would like to see more readily available to more students. There are also a growing number of innovative projects that seek to effect change within the existing educational models, for example, the Harmony Project.[10] This inspiring, pioneering program aims to teach children (and their teachers) how we are all connected to nature and how to live together more peacefully and sustainably. The Harmony Project is a charitable organization led by Richard Dunne. It was inspired by the book *Harmony: A New Way of Looking at Our World*[11] by HRH the Prince of Wales. It provides schools and educators with a framework that aims to put Nature's principles at the heart of teaching and learning.

It was the Harmony Project that inspired me to run a project on a local care farm that we affectionately nicknamed

---

10   For more information on The Harmony Project, go to www.theharmonyproject.org.uk

11   HRH The Prince of Wales, *Harmony: A New Way of Looking at Our World*

'Farmony.' The project aimed to introduce home-educating families to the Harmony principles within the context of the farm and through the three key areas of harmony with self, with others, and with Nature. The potential for this and other such projects to build the bridges between the old and the new paradigms is exciting, and I'm heartened to see the Harmony Project going from strength to strength.

So, how can we, as parents and educators, facilitate this shift?

I believe a necessary starting point is to rethink how we raise our children, as parents, educators, and communities. We need to shift our perception of who children are, our relationships with them, and our role in their lives. Children don't belong to us. They are not 'ours' to control. Yet, if we're lucky, we have the privilege of supporting, protecting, and nurturing them for a short period.

Crucially, parents and educators must understand how our current education system creates and feeds into the dominant way of thinking and living that underpins our existing societal structures. This realization will help expand the understanding that education is not something that needs to be 'done to children.' Life *is* education. It doesn't need to be separate. We can learn what we need to know when we need to learn it, and there is no need for prescriptive curricula, testing, and exams.

A key part of this shift is to understand the illusions about life and work. For example, most of us believe we need to work hard at school to get a good job, so we can continue to work hard until we retire. One justification for sending children to school for much of their childhood is to facilitate parents' work, a means of educational childcare.

But do we really need to spend much of our adult lives working (for many of us, we work simply as a means of paying our bills and providing for our families?) Anthropologist David Graeber puts forward an interesting perspective on the work-life conundrum. [12] He contends that over half of modern-day jobs are actually pointless and that many could be done in a fraction of the time.

Graeber is not the only person to be voicing these thoughts. With the changes in work demands and patterns over recent years, many people are questioning the need to be chained to their desks for large chunks of time and are calling for a shift to a more balanced way of life.

I appreciate this is not a quick and easy shift to make. We live in a society where money is the main way of meeting many of our needs, and we are primarily entrenched in the nine-to-five, five-days-a-week working model, but we are beginning to see that there could be other ways, and as more people open their eyes to new possibilities, changes will start to happen.

Communication is key

To create change, I believe we need to understand how we are perpetuating the competitive, right/wrong, separation paradigm through the violent way in which most of us are conditioned to communicate. Although we may not perceive how we communicate as being violent, think about how we often speak

---

12   Graeber, David, *Bullshit Jobs*

to our children. If they have a meltdown, they're chastised for being difficult or naughty; if they answer back or refuse to do something, they're accused of being rude, demanding, and challenging. Children learn by modeling behavior. Adults consistently model the behavior they don't wish to see in their children and then blame them for misbehaving.

This way of interacting with children stems from the old control-comply paradigm of child rearing and is reinforced by parenting 'experts' and educationalists the world over. Although there has been a move towards 'carrot' rather than 'stick' (rewards rather than punishment) methods of child-rearing and schooling over recent years, much of the popular advice still seems to me, in some form or another, a version of 'How to get your kids to... [insert here what you will, e.g., listen, sit still, go to bed on time, be nice to their sibling, etc.]' The underlying assumption is that children need training, taming, and pacifying, and that if they don't comply, there is something wrong with them or the adult 'in charge.'

What's more, as parents and teachers, we often make judgmental comments about children's behavior. These may be made with the best intentions at heart, a desire to encourage or to motivate, to steer or to correct. Or they may be borne out of anger, when, in the heat of the moment, we are triggered by something a child says or does and the words just spill out, unchecked.

When we are triggered, we tend to blame others for our emotional reactions to their behavior, thinking they are at fault because *we* feel like this when *they* do that. These automatic responses are based on learned, repeated patterns first formed in childhood. In fact, our thoughts, actions, and feelings are rarely based upon the truth of the situation we see in front of us. Instead, they are based upon our judgements about what we are observing.

How we respond to our children usually depends on what we are telling ourselves about their behavior, drawing on our own past experiences, often learned patterns from our own parents. So, how we treat and speak to our children is mostly a consequence of all that's come before. It's a self-perpetuating cycle.

Marshall Rosenberg (founder of the Center for Nonviolent Communication) referred to this type of judging, blaming, thinking, and communicating as jackal behavior. The jackal's life-alienating way of communicating is not (as I used to believe) simply the way humans are. Instead, it is a common symptom of our modern society, a consequence of the right and wrong mentality that we are conditioned into from birth.

Thankfully, there is a flip side to the jackal: the giraffe. The language of the giraffe is life-enhancing; it's how we communicate when we are connected with the inner compassionate nature that Rosenberg believed (as do I) is inside us all. Those of you who tend to rely more on the reward and positive feedback style of communicating with the children in your care (as was my default strategy until more recent years) may be surprised to learn this is also regarded as jackal communication [13]. In fact, any language or behavior designed (whether consciously or unconsciously) to coerce another person into doing what we want them to do is a form of jackal communication.

---

13   For more on the surprising impacts of motivating children by rewards, see Kohn, Alfie, *Punished by Rewards*

As an assertive-discipline-trained, sticker-chart-loving teacher and parent, it took me some time to get to grips with this concept. I just didn't see anything wrong with praising and rewarding children, and I couldn't imagine how else to control a class of students without resorting to less favorable measures!

Releasing the old paradigm

Over time, my view changed as I came to realize that this perceived need to control is a symptom of the old separation paradigm of living. This realization led me to consider: what if parenting and educating weren't about getting children to do what the adults want them to do? What if, instead of spending our time and energy trying to control children, we did less, trusted more, and allowed them to be...well, children?!

It's a hard habit to break, but I believe we need to break it if we want to bring about change. So, how do we do this? We begin by reconnecting with our inner giraffes, by understanding that we are all compassionate beings at heart and that behind everyone's jackal is a loving, wonderful 'giraffe' just waiting to come out.

Fundamental to this is understanding the connection between our needs, feelings, thoughts, and words (or actions). Like Rosenberg, I believe that our behavior is an effort to meet our needs. So, if we can uncover the needs behind the jackal words and behavior, we can gain a greater understanding of what is going on for the other person, and we can more readily empathize with them.

From this place of empathy, we have a choice: either to continue in jackal mode, with our judging and blaming language, or to step into our giraffe skin and communicate from the heart. This may sound simple in theory, but I know from experience that it takes some getting to grips with – especially if your jackal has been very loud for many years, as mine has.

Crucially, we need to transform how we communicate with ourselves, to learn, what for many of us are, the long-lost skills of self-empathy and self-compassion. Moreover, I believe that, if we can open our eyes to the systemic reasons behind the jackal behaviors, in ourselves and others, then it is easier to see that it is not our fault; in fact, it is nobody's fault. In so doing, it becomes easier to release our blame and guilt and open our hearts to love. Naturally, it is so much easier to love and accept others if we can first learn to love and accept ourselves.

If we can learn to love ourselves unconditionally, we will be more readily able to love our children unconditionally too. As we start to shift from judgment, blame, and separation towards acceptance, compassion, and connection, so will our children. Consequently, our children will grow into loving, compassionate adults, who will instinctively raise their children that way too…And in so doing, we will break the cycle.

Closing thoughts

I believe we are all born with the seeds of our infinite potential glowing brightly inside our souls. We are all born with innate wisdom as loving, accepting, compassionate beings.

As the years go by, the glow becomes fainter and fainter until, for many of us, it fizzles out and dies, leaving behind the shell of what we could have been.

For some of us, the embers are rekindled, often decades later when, perhaps dissatisfied with the path our life has taken or triggered by a major life-changing event, we get a sense or hear a voice, a whisper inside us that nudges us to make a shift, a change, to do something different.

How would it be if we didn't have to endure decades of struggle to find our true purpose, our inner calling?

What if, instead of micro-managing our children, we simply allowed them to be the wise, infinite, loving, curious souls that we all are?

What if education was not about competition, right/wrong, or success/failure?

What if it was about learning to communicate with self and others compassionately?

What if the arts, sports, creativity, and self-expression were valued as highly as mathematics, English, and science?

What if, instead of spending years of their lives memorizing and regurgitating facts, children were given the space and freedom to discover the joys of life?

What if they were trusted to find out for themselves the things that truly *set their souls on fire?*

Children already know how to learn. They don't need us to show them. Babies are born into this world, ready to explore and discover. Young children already know what adults have long forgotten and spend much of their later years striving to rediscover.

Sometimes, when I look at the state the world is in and think about how far away we are from the new paradigm, I feel overwhelmed, hopeless, and despondent. Does this sound familiar? If so, take heart. Remember, we don't have to do it alone, nor do we need to do it all now. We only need to take one step at a time, and that step will be different for every one of us.

We are living through a time of great transition, and we all have an essential part to play in this transformation. We are the bridging generation. The old is breaking down, and the new is being birthed. Like any birth, the labor may be long and hard, but the result will be magical. Something never before witnessed on this planet. The most significant change needs to come from each of us as individuals.

We all have the power within us. We just need to let go of the fear and shake ourselves free from the conditioning. Instead of asking how, trying to rationalize it, or figuring it out, we need to connect with our inner guidance and trust in life. Crucially, we must empower our children to do this too.

As more of us start to do so, we will create a ripple effect, and as these ripples grow, we will shift into a new paradigm, a paradigm of connection, compassion, and love.

"Learning to create space for your highest good, to dance, to do yoga, breathwork, meditation, journaling, art, and so much more are all keys to this new paradigm we have entered together."

~ Meka Leach

CHAPTER THIRTEEN

I Believe and Trust in Myself - Mindfulness Education

By: Meka Leach, Age 13

I was just four years old when I was invited to train with an Olympic fencer. On that day, I was playing basketball with my best friend. Our parents had looked at the local park district to put us in a class together, so they could carpool. Little did we know the basketball coach was a fencer too. The coach would follow my mom to the car after each practice saying I should try fencing. To be honest, my mom didn't even really know what fencing was. There was a local tournament coming up, and my mom said I could watch and tell the coach thank you, but no thank you. My mom always thought I was the princess who would want tea parties and dress-up. When we arrived at the tournament, my mom thought I would hate it. She even coached me on what to say to my basketball coach. She told me to say, "Thank you for thinking of me, but this is definitely not me."

When we arrived, the gym was filled with shouting and the clanking of swords. The atmosphere was incredible. Seeing the action and feeling the tension in the room, my whole body tingled as I took it all in. *Girls can sword fight?* Without hesitation, I told my mom I wanted to fence! My parents were so supportive of my dreams that naturally they said yes. To their surprise, I loved fencing just as much as I loved playing with my dolls. From that moment, it had my heart. I was focused, persistent, and trained for over twenty-five hours a week at the age of five. I was taking five classes and five private lessons a week, driving to a fencing club that was over an hour away to practice. At first, I was in public school, trying to find the balance between school, training hard, traveling at a super young age, and competing. But when I was in second grade, my parents decided to let me try homeschooling so I could follow my passion. I had the time and energy to focus on fencing, which formed most of my curriculum. Fencing, alongside mindfulness, were both great teachers to me.

I vividly remember, at age ten, being in a national fencing championship. My body was trembling as I knew every move had to be perfect if I wanted to win. I felt the power running through my soul with every movement and breath I made. My sword was no longer separate from my body; we had become one. I knew that I had the power and strength to become the national champion, I reminded myself, as sweat was gushing like a waterfall from every pore on my body. The packed gym was silent. I paused…. took a huge breath and chanted the affirmation, *"I believe and trust myself."* Once those words vibrated through every cell in my body, I was ready.

We were in the last few minutes of the match when I realized that I was losing. I could hear my coach yelling at me in the background of the noisy gym. But his words were a blur, and my mind was already lost in the aftermath of the match. I was too worried about losing and wasn't being *present* in each moment. Finally, I came back to the precious moment of *now*. I said, *"I know I can do this,"* even when my nerves felt like they were getting the better of me. *"No matter how hard it is, I know I have to keep it together. I am the champion of this match. I am not giving up."*

With only ten seconds left, I was just one point down. I was no longer scared or worried. This moment was *all* I had. I had trained like an Olympian for many years to be here. I heard the referee say, "Ready, fence!" I fleshed, making my body become an arrow pointed straight at my opponent's body, using every muscle to move forward as fast as possible and scoring a point that tied up the score and put us into overtime. I walked back to my start line, staying present, thinking of as many affirmations as I could say. I felt my breath coming out of my body like a warm breeze at the beach. I felt my hand and sword strong and ready. Once again, I heard the words, "Ready, fence." I waited for the other fencer to come to me. Pausing, I used the momentum of the energy in the room. I blocked her sword and attacked, hitting her and seeing my light go off. I was victorious! I had just become the National Youth Fencing Champion Epee Girls at ten years old.

That moment transformed me into the person I am today. I learned the power of affirmations and believing in yourself. After winning the championship, I realized my journey on the fencing strip was over. It was so clear that I was living in fear of what everyone would think of me if I quit fencing; everyone was always saying I was the face to beat. They told me I would be the next Olympian, meant for greatness in the fencing community. The day I walked into the cold gym where I had trained countless hours to become the champion, the room was dark, stale, and gloomy. I remember sitting down across from my coach and my mom. My coach looked deep into my eyes and told me I was a quitter for leaving the fencing world. He told me, if I quit now, I would always be a quitter. Call it as you wish, but fencing was just no longer a part of my journey, and I accepted it with pride. I looked back in my coach's eyes, thanked him for his time and loyalty to me through the years, and walked out of that gym with my head high. I live my legacy now in the moment of what is right, not self-sabotaging my journey to be accepted by others.

I spent many days, weeks, and months diving deep and rediscovering who I was at age ten. I discovered my journey and purpose, giving myself the grace to find Meka the person, not the fencer. I discovered I am here to spread the beautiful light of love and help change my generation and future generations in a new paradigm of education. Fencing was the pinpoint I needed in my journey to feel and know the power of loving and believing in myself. Life is precious and should be abundant with love and gratitude.

When my passion turned more within, I discovered mindfulness. I still remember my first yoga class and sound journey, walking into the large empty room without knowing what to expect, other than it sounded fun and something my mom and I could do together. This led me to want to learn more. Again, like fencing, the desire to be a part of this new practice was instant. I turned to my mom and told her

I wanted to become a yoga teacher. She laughed and said, "That's great, sweetie. I wanted to be a taxicab driver when I was young." I adamantly replied, "No, Mom, It's not like that. I am *meant* to do the training to become a yoga teacher." To see if I was serious or not, my parents agreed that, if I could come up with half the tuition, they would pay the other. I started making earrings and jewelry to raise funds.

After one class, I told my teacher how I was meant to become a yoga teacher and that I had a huge calling from the universe to take on the training. To my surprise, the yoga teacher and the owners of the amazing sanctuary offered to pay my half of the tuition so that I could start the training! In the weeks that followed, with divine timing, I took nine months of school on top of my regular homeschooling to become a certified yoga teacher. Then I studied to become a Reiki master, becoming the first 10-year-old in the world to do it.

I now have the wisdom and knowledge I learned on the strip as a fencer to help me develop classes alongside all I have learned through yoga teacher training, Reiki, and other modalities I have studied. I'm passionate about finding new ways to bring mindfulness to my peers and adults, which is necessary for this new paradigm of education, for example, taking the time to write and develop classes to prepare young menstruators for when the universe gives them the powerful sacred force of bringing life into this world.

Most kids I teach are between seven and fourteen years old, but I teach adult classes too. I also offer online mindfulness classes for young ones. What I love most is seeing my students walk out of my class more confident and ready for the journey the universe has for them. I am grateful to have this freedom in my life, where I can balance mindfulness teaching alongside my homeschooling.

I believe that teaching kids to love all their flaws and embrace and be proud of who they are is so important, as well as taking time to build the skills of forgiveness to yourself and others. It is also essential to end deep-rooted trauma lines that can be passed down from generation to generation. Making sure we learn to care for our physical and mental bodies is also part of mindfulness. Learning to create space for your highest good, to dance, to do yoga, breathwork, meditation, journaling, art, and so much more are all keys to this new paradigm we have entered together.

Resource: Mindfulness with Meka

Now, I challenge you to print these affirmations and hang them by your child's bed or in their bathroom. Be the annoying parent to read it aloud to them whenever you walk by this paper. They might roll their eyes. They might scream. They might sit and be embarrassed, BUT DO IT! Inside, they will be *smiling*. Inside, they will feel your *love*. We need to hear these things. So go ahead and plant the seeds. We might be crabby, but please don't give up...

Affirmations: You can switch "I am" to "You are."

- I AM KIND

- I AM A GREAT LISTENER

- I AM SAFE

- I AM HELPFUL

- I AM BRAVE

- I HAVE MANY GIFTS AND TALENTS

- I MAKE A POSITIVE DIFFERENCE IN THE WORLD

- I AM SMART

- I AM UNIQUE

- I TRUST MYSELF

- I AM LOVED

- I CAN DO IT

- I AM LIMITLESS

- I BELIEVE IN MYSELF

- I WILL FACE MY FEARS

- I AM ENOUGH

- I AM ALWAYS WILLING TO LEARN

- I AM THANKFUL

"If education was defined as a 'system,' let it be in accordance with the system of the Earth and all her creatures great or small, the alignment of the stars, the beating of your heart and the abundance of nature."

~ Monique Sayers

CHAPTER FOURTEEN

Holistic Education of the Earth, Body, Mind, Soul and the Rise in Ascension

By Monique Sayers

"If we surrendered to Earth's intelligence, we could rise up rooted, like trees."

- Rilke

She must have known. Of course, she did! As I lay in my room, preparing to sleep, I channeled light from the Quantum in an evening meditation when my five-year-old daughter Coral angelically bounced in.

"Mama, will you massage me as I fall asleep?" Coral asked eagerly.

"Of course," I answered curiously.

Surprisingly, Coral pointed toward her forehead (third eye) and the back of her neck rather than a more commonplace for massage, such as her back. As part of my meditation, I channeled energy to my pituitary gland, which I accessed by touching my forehead and back of the neck lightly with my fingers. With fingers lit up like golden rods of sunlight, I gently massaged Coral. It was clear at this moment that she did know! She was awakened, a Starseed of light here to shine brightly on Earth. Though more than any label, she was a unique, regular child of this world, curious to be, do, and explore whatever she wanted, and I was there for her every moment.

"Can you feel it? The light?" I asked Coral.

"Yes, Mama," she replied knowingly, as her eyes gently closed into the starry night. No more words were necessary. This was not the first time Coral had shown me her connection to the light, but what was surprising was her precision in knowing the exact anchor points on my body that I was working on without her being physically in the room.

"Of course, she *knew,*" I realized. Coral often bounced into my room when I was hosting meditation classes, as the frequency would heighten. I always smiled at these moments, grateful she was open to receiving and giving the vibrations. It wasn't the first time we had connected through the mind, body, and soul, from birth to ascension and beyond.

As an educator, mother, and custodian of Earth, I have experienced education in many ways. Nothing is separate. We are all connected through evolution. So, it was no surprise that Coral could feel "my" energy, as it was part of the collective energy within the Quantum Field. Knowing that *everything* is interconnected, education, therefore, is holistic. So, can we apply holistic education to our students or children? The answer to this question starts from *within.*

Holistic education is not about choosing one path or another; rather, it comes from oneness consciousness, meaning everything is connected and in divine order. Holistic education is nothing new. It's an ancient evolution, like a crystal of light containing the wisdom of the Earth ready to heal, guide, and co-create with us or a toroid that spirals, constantly evolving, changing and overflowing with abundance. From a Quantum perspective, education is received and shared through a frequency of light like a web of connection. I invite you to also consider education not only as a three-dimensional object, such as "school," and instead envision it as a living, evolving consciousness that is five-dimensional and beyond.

If education was defined as a "system," let it be in accordance with the system of the Earth and all her creatures, great or small, the alignment of the stars, the beating of your heart, and the abundance of nature. Let it flow like a waterfall, an abundance of water trickling into the Earth's veins serving us all collectively, rather than being drawn person by person from the smallness of a rigid, artificial, dried-up dam. Nothing is separate; we are all one. Knowing this is great education. I imagine education that flows following natural cycles, the elements, light language, soul-aligned education, sacred geometry, outdoors/indoor learning, and self-care. I imagine lessons guided by the stars and great reverence to divine order, which nature brings forth. I invite you to consider what ignites your views on holistic education.

Gandhi[14] described holistic education as being of the head, hands, and heart. For example, if a child (or adult for that

---

14   Shukla, Ramakant, *Gandhian Philosophy of Education*, Sublime Publications: Jaipur, 2002.

matter) is tired, emotional, hungry, or not feeling safe, this affects the child's body, mind, and soul as a whole eco-system. It all comes back to being regulated[15], as learning happens when the neurons of the amygdala (emotions), hippocampus (learning and memory), and prefrontal cortex (self-regulation) are calm and not disconnected from the body. There are thousands of different models, research, and practices that reflect holistic learning as the alignment of the body (The Chakras[16]), mind (Maslow's Hierarchy of Needs.[17]), Earth and soul (Quantum Planes of Existence.)

"All things in nature are not only one with themselves
but also one with totality."

- Ekhart Tolle

Let's look at how the brain is designed to serve the needs of the body, environment, and emotions before moving into learning and self-actualization. You can imagine the brain as a tree going from root to rise, in correlation with the Chakras. It starts with the reptilian brain designed for the Physiological (root chakra) and Safety (sacral chakra) needs of a person and moves up into the mammalian brain, which is the center for Love and Belonging (solar plexus) and Self-Esteem (heart chakra). The highest part of the brain branches into Self-Actualization,

---

15   Chiesa, A., & Serretti, A. (2010). A systematic review of neurobiological and clinical features of mindfulness meditations. *Psychological Medicine, 40*(8), pp. 1239-1252.

16   McMurray, Suzanne BSN, RN, CSMC. Chakra Talk: Exploring Human Energy Systems. *Holistic Nursing Practice, 19*(2), p. 94.

17   Silton, Nava & Flannelly, Laura & Flannelly, Kevin & Galek, Kathleen. (2011). Toward a Theory of Holistic Needs and the Brain. *Holistic Nursing Practice*, 25. pp. 258-65. 10.1097/HNP.0b013e31822a0301.

which includes cognitive (throat chakra), actualization (third-eye chakra), and transcendence (crown chakra). This interconnectivity in receiving information shows that learning happens in a state of wholeness. Therefore, connecting deeply with our emotions and multi-dimensional experiences as a human is the ultimate school. Life is, in fact, school! Knowing this, can you imagine creating a system for education that is out of balance with our natural state of consciousness?

The old paradigm of education focused on the Intelligence Quotient (IQ) as a standard measure of intelligence, yet this is out of order with the evolution of the whole brain system. By honoring our emotional intelligence (EQ) and energetic intelligence (EnQ),[18] it's possible to rise into a higher state of consciousness. This is where learning happens[19]. Holistic education is a state of consciousness that, when activated, brings curiosity, joy, and all kinds of learning. It's a pleasure to witness students and adults in this state of happiness, where *anything is possible*! When children are calm, they can use their minds for whatever kinds of learning they desire. For example, my daughter Coral loves drawing, writing, counting, bike-riding, playing in the sand, and dressing up, and she is always curious to learn and explore everything. I welcome all of it!

By embodying education of the highest frequency of light, we can support future generations of children as our collective imprint serves as a "model" of education. As we are transforming, so too is education. Wholeness is where suffering ends and enlightenment appears as an ever-evolving

---

18   Jeroslow, C. *A New Paradigm of Education*, 2021.
19   Thierry, K., Bryant, H; Nobles, S. et al. (2016). Two-Year Impact of a Mindfulness-Based Program on Preschoolers' Self-Regulation and Academic Performance. *Early Education and Development*, 5(1), pp. 1-11.

dance of life. This dance leads to great wisdom and connection to self, others, and the Earth. This is how we rise into a new paradigm of education.

"We are hardwired to connect with others, it's what gives purpose and meaning to our lives, and without it, there is suffering."

- Brené Brown

I wish to share with you some Quantum, Energy, Mindfulness, and Meditation tools and resources designed to balance the brain's hemispheres and open the gateways to a beautiful state of awakening. By now, you have learned that, by being regulated, all other learning can take place. I invite you to explore the depth of these tools as direct transmissions of light. You will find real-life experiences about my daughter, students, children, and adults with whom I have co-created. They are not listed in any order of the mind, body, earth, soul, or ascension, as the experience brings forth the connected sense of learning or wholeness. Being a student of the light has educated my whole being, and it is my sincere wish that something ignites within you as well.

1. Design Your Life: What's your vision for a new paradigm of education?

I invite you to do this exercise to clarify what kind of education you feel you are aligned with using visioning techniques. You can also use the technique for other visions you may have. Focus on one at a time.

I have connected with educators, mentors, parents, business owners, and intuitive beings from all around the world through our podcast, *A New Paradigm of Education*, where we talk about their vision for the future of education, which is already happening now. I have found that, while there is not a one-size-fits-all "system," the podcast guests all share a common thread of wanting to innovate education by considering what is best for each unique child, as well as the highest good of humanity.

In general terms, the old system of schooling was to send children all day to match parents' routines, who also chose a 9-5 role. However, since this paradigm shift, I have witnessed a change whereby people are choosing to follow their passions, take time for life, and design what suits their lifestyle.

Humanity's consciousness has risen, with many people ready to step into a New Earth or A New Paradigm of Education. So, what does that look like for you and the greater good of humanity?

Each of us has a role that will both align with our higher selves and support children. It may be taking a small step, exploring what is possible, birthing a new school, stepping away from all that doesn't serve you, connecting with other change-makers, offering a course or your unique gifts, or taking a quantum leap into a fifth-dimensional school. So, I invite you to play, enjoy, relax, and expand your consciousness, to know there are limitless options within the Quantum field when you visualize what you wish for this new paradigm of education.

Here are some real-life examples of people I've met, who are walking their paths toward a new paradigm of education in their own ways.

☐ I have interviewed unschooling families whose absolute dream is to be immersed with their children all day. Why would they want to be apart and miss precious moments?

☐ I have met with mothers who are burned out and value self-care as an essential aspect of this new paradigm. Often, they collaborate with other families and homeschool together by having some days on or off.

☐ I have met a range of people who have set up forest schools, New Earth schools, or unstructured communities that allow families to come and go according to their desires and routines. Set days are not required; why not use the cycles of the Earth as a guide for time? For example, the new moon, eclipses, etc.

☐ Some people have remained in regular schools but are activating changes through policy or changes within their homes and, most importantly, within themselves.

☐ I've seen projects birthed with community members offering their gifts or areas of specialty, which support children's values, intuition, innovation, and life as key for learning. This might either be part of a "school" or their own form of education, for example, tree education, crystals, ayurveda, dolphins, life skills, information technology, or gratitude.

☐ I'm part of Magic School run by the Oneness Foundation, which is a multi-dimensional school of light where we offer classes to kids or teens in the Quantum, such as "Wand Magic," "Meditation," "Spirit-Animals," and "Light Language."

☐ I've seen mobile schools where students travel around Hawaii in a van to different portals or energy power centers and allow the wisdom of the land to educate them.

☐ How about homeschooling hubs? You can drop off your child to a mentor or be there all day with your child. These are highly flexible, and you could use a curriculum or simply allow life to be a curriculum.

☐ Flexi-schooling is a similar option, where school days are interspersed with planned days off for a better balance of time with the family.

☐ Self-directed learning and entrepreneurship have sky-rocketed, and I have met with many teens who are already authors or have soul-aligned businesses. This is the new paradigm of youth!

☐ There are limitless options, and perhaps, there will be many you try as you work towards your vision.

Your turn: *What's your vision for this new paradigm of education?*

☐ Close your eyes for a few minutes.

☐ Take some long, deep breaths, exhaling more slowly than you inhale.

☐ Imagine yourself feeling grounded, your feet sinking deeply into the Earth.

☐ Take another breath and move up your body with a spiraling cord of golden light past the top of your head into the sky. Keep going higher and higher.

- ☐ Welcome your higher self and your guides as you land on a cloud of white light.

- ☐ Take another breath and fully relax in the clouds, allowing them to hold you.

- ☐ Now ask yourself, "What do I need to see at this moment that will support a new paradigm of education?" (You could adapt this as applicable.)

- ☐ Allow yourself to receive any answers through visions, words, codes, symbols, feelings, colors, or whatever else comes in.

- ☐ If nothing is present, stay with that. Trust that you will receive the answers you have asked for later, if not now.

- ☐ Once you feel complete, say thank you. Being grateful supports the fruition of miracles.

- ☐ When you feel ready, return to your body.

- ☐ You may do this practice on repeat.

- ☐ Take a rest, draw, or write your vision, depending on what feels aligned.

- ☐ Share it! A new paradigm of education is about co-creation, connection, and collaboration.

- ☐ If you feel guided to know precisely how to activate this template of visioning, you can reach out to me or any other mentor you feel guided to create with.

Chakras[20], Brain and Planes of Existence show the interconnection of the mind, body and soul.

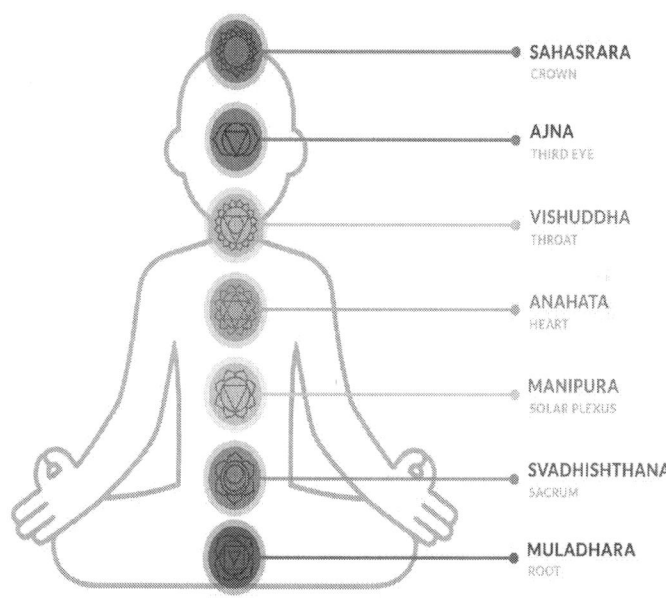

SAHASRARA
CROWN

AJNA
THIRD EYE

VISHUDDHA
THROAT

ANAHATA
HEART

MANIPURA
SOLAR PLEXUS

SVADHISHTHANA
SACRUM

MULADHARA
ROOT

---

20   Human chakras infographic chart: License #175856322

5 MAJOR BRAIN FUNCTIONS

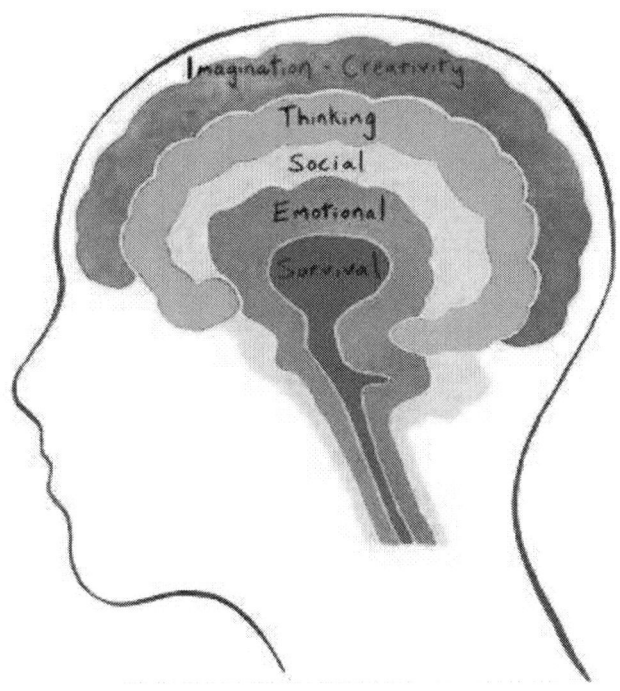

---

21   This drawing was created to replace Maclean's triune brain model by
      Mark Waldman, Monica Evason and brain tumor survivors from www.
      successcharity.org in the UK. Permission granted.

2. Cosmic Dreaming and Activations

Here are some channeled meditations for children, activating their connection with guides, animals, nature, light language, crystals, as well as body and breath awareness.

Here are some real-life examples of energy sessions that my daughter and I have channeled together. They are appropriate for a child around five years old, but you could adjust these accordingly.

☐ "Light-Hearted Activation": Hug heart to heart. Send a golden cord of light connecting your hearts and visualize the energy running back and forth between your heart centers. Ask the child: Do you see any colors? Can you feel a rod of light? What else do you experience?

☐ "Energy Blessing": Imagine your fingers or hands are filled with golden light. Send this golden light to your food, plants, or others. You can ask the child what they wish to bless. I sometimes add a chant-like OM to make it fun and amplify the light. This is a blessing of light, so the more you practice, the more the connection with their guides will develop.

☐ When children make sounds of animals or noises, perhaps they are activating us with light language. I will often join in when my daughter makes sounds and send light at the same time as receiving it. Play is the doorway to the divine.

☐ "Lion's Breath": Breathe in and then, as you exhale, "roar" like a lion. The animal or sound you choose could change, for example, to a bear, dolphin, etc. You can invite a connection to a spirit animal that the child could develop over time. You also ask the child to hold their stomach as they breathe, so they learn body awareness.

☐ "Bubble of light": Imagine you are inside a bubble of light. It is magnificent and covers your whole body and aura. How does it feel? Are you happy? You can pop it and come out again when you wish. When the child is ready, this could be developed over time as a Quantum Tool for restoration or protection.

☐ "Prayer": This is not necessarily about being religious (though it can be); it is about learning how to be grateful, create miracles, and build a relationship with the universe, guides, the divine, or nature. Design the prayer with an affirmative frame, send it off on a balloon of light, and allow it to return in divine order.

☐ "Crystal Magic": There are many kinds of activations with crystals, in their physical and energetic form. I have used them to develop emotional skills, like having a rock friend who supports the child, gives healing, and works with them in delivering messages. I have placed crystals in nature to "find" children. Crystals find you. My daughter is learning how to care for them and experimenting with healing through interaction. I have allowed her to develop her interaction with them to see what she will discover for herself.

☐ "Sacred Geometry" is everywhere in nature: snowflakes, flower petals, crystals, shells, the stars, the galaxy we spiral within, the air we breathe, even our eye corneas, the grid lines, and multi-dimensionality aspects of the Quantum field. The spiral below represents energy and the evolution of the soul and a Fibonacci sequence in math. The pyramids and other sacred places were built with sacred geometry. I have been to the Oneness University, Ekam, in India, a powerful geometrical temple of light. With my daughter, we used a crystal pendulum over different shapes to experiment with the direction of energy and physics and to build a connection with crystals as a living consciousness. You could also get into nature with your students or children and see what you can find. Nature is sacred. Enjoy.

3. The Little Buddha Under a Tree

(You can call this exercise whatever you like, the little unicorn, the little snow angel, etc.)

Here is a channeled story that can be used for sleep, meditation, or visualization with children to connect with their higher selves, animal spirit, guides, and the Quantum dimension.

The story below is something I channeled with my daughter. It activates the column of ascension or three hearts connection between the Earth heart in the core of Mother Gaia, the physical heart of the child, and their soul star in the sky. It also acts as a safe place to return to each day, as the setting is always under a tree, and we always imagine traveling to the clouds. You could offer this as a meditation, but my daughter and I do this when she is lying down ready to sleep. She usually falls asleep when we reach the clouds, and we go to the Astral dream realm. You could instead use the clouds as a portal for manifesting by connecting with their chosen power animal or the divine. I always ensure that we return to Earth, even if she is asleep, so it is a grounded and safe practice. I invite her to travel again through the dimensions if she chooses to do so. This story works well for my daughter at age five. Feel free to create your inspired version.

The Bodhi Tree is the name of the tree the Buddha sat under when he was enlightened and became very happy. What's the name of your tree? You can hug trees in real life and receive positive energy. Always ask them for permission to do so. You can also draw your tree with your favorite light colors, guides, and animal friends.

Storytime:

"Once upon a time, there was a little buddha under a golden tree. What a beautiful tree it was. She felt like her feet were sinking into the tree's roots, getting lower and lower, and spiraling down into the Earth. There was a cord of light spinning through her, spinning like she was traveling down into the sacred heart of mother Gaia. What a magnificent place it was, connected with beautiful crystal light. She then traveled back up the golden cord of light to the golden tree. She walked around the tree and was greeted by a special winged friend (unicorn, lion, dragon, Blue Avian etc.)

"Can you see your unicorn? What color is it? Very good. The unicorn said it would fly up into the clouds, and you could join it if you want to. Put your hands on your heart and feel if it says yes. Breathe in. Breathe out.

"It's time to go. If you're ready, hop onto the unicorn's back. It's time to fly, higher and higher, as high as the clouds. You can fly higher and higher again. It's time to arrive. You can get off your unicorn and step onto the clouds. How nice does it feel! It's luminous white with sparkles of joy. How peaceful and relaxing. This is a place you can go in your dreams and travel anywhere in the universe. If you feel ready to dream, ask your unicorn to take you on an adventure. You can enter the dream realm and fly anywhere together. If you want to stay in the soft clouds, relax here. You can connect with the stars, too. Your soul star is here. Enjoy.

"When you're ready, hop back onto your unicorn and travel down the spiraling light. Down, down, down until you reach the magical tree, feeling its luminous leaves on your feet. Now keep traveling back down until your feet are on the Earth again. Very good. You see the little buddha and feel one with it. You touch your heart and say thank you to your unicorn. See you another day. Your unicorn is ready to sleep. You can too."

2. When Math Turns into Mindfulness

I was guiding a student with one-on-one math sessions. I felt aligned to do so, as he loves math and always showed up enthusiastic, wanting to know more. It was not forced upon him, like in the old paradigm of rigid learning or control. Math for Billy[22] was like art or sport for another student. He loved it and was sharing his gift with the world. However, in this session, he was unusually distracted and feeling anxious. We started with a few questions, but he looked distant instead of with his usual curiosity.

"What's on your mind today, Billy?" I asked compassionately.

He replied, "It's the cross-country. I can't stop thinking about it."

"Why is that so?" I asked.

"Well, I feel so nervous. I'm going to Nationals, and I want to win," Billy replied.

---

22   The name Billy is a pseudonym.

I then realized that the best way I could support him would be through meditation. I was sure this would be something "new" to him, so I approached it as an invitation for him to decide upon. First, I asked him to close his eyes for one minute with his permission. Then, I offered a safe place for him to visualize himself running on the track and imagine himself coming towards the end of the race and feeling happy, regardless of the outcome, and with a desire to do his best. Finally, I explained that he could always come back to this place and visualize it again at any moment.

(Note: I did not feel aligned to ask him to visualize winning, as it's important that I was not influencing his decisions. But, of course, if he naturally envisioned this, then this outcome is possible.)

The next session, Billy was beaming when he arrived. He explained that he came second at Nationals. He even mentioned that the visualization helped him feel calm and have a place to focus. I was so happy for him. Of course, his training would have supported his running as well, but what helped his nerves was practicing this one-minute visualization.

One-minute Visualization for Kids/Teens

☐ If you want, please close your eyes. This is the place where you can make your dreams come true.

☐ Sit up straight and feel your hands in your lap.

☐ Take in one breath and out one breath. In, out. Very good.

- ☐ Imagine yourself … (for example, running on the track.) Then, have a look around at what you see and what you hear.

- ☐ Now imagine yourself feeling so happy (while on the track.)

- ☐ This is your dream. You can choose what you want to do in it. I will give you a few seconds to enjoy it.

- ☐ When ready, wiggle your hands and toes and open your eyes.

- ☐ You are welcome to share with me, draw a picture, or write down your experience.

If you feel guided, Monique would love to support you or your children at anewparadigmofeducation@gmail.com.

"A New Paradigm of Education is like a fractal of ice that shatters and reforms into a flowing stream; it has the same molecular structure, yet it now has a new purpose and a greater evolution."

~ Monique Sayers

CONCLUSION: CLOSING CEREMONY

A Reflection On Some Key Themes

A New Paradigm of Education Rising is greater than us; it's a collective field of radical change in education that serves the highest good of all. Each of our stories forms part of a library of light being created, expanded upon, deleted, and upgraded as it evolves from one paradigm to the next that was co-created along with you. While each author shared their unique gifts and knowledge within this book, there were some overarching key messages that form an interconnected web of wisdom.

A key theme was the holistic education of body, mind, and soul in alignment with Earth. Each author shared that, for the mind to be truly educated, it must also be synchronized with the heart, soul, and body. We are not saying never to use the mind, but that learning is also affected or created by the body, the soul's choices, the feelings in the heart, and the environment a child or student is in. There is no one-size-fits-all model but rather a kaleidoscope filled with various colors, perspectives, and visions. We invite you to consider what holistic education means for you, your students, and your children.

The notion of us all *rising* into the best version of ourselves is another theme throughout the chapters included in this book. We expressed how serving students and children with an empty cup is a disservice. Some chapters offered direct guidance on how to become regulated, have our needs met, and more importantly, become role models of holistic education by showing up as the best versions of ourselves. Other chapters offered direct services for children who may need therapy or more profound work, which also supports the entire family unit to rise. We are not saying we need to be superhumans, but rather to do our tasks gently and lovingly and be the best that we can be at each moment. It's a lifetime's journey right there!

A number of chapters in this book also explored the idea of rising in terms of bringing together a collective field of consciousness. If we can show up with more awakened truth and joy, this has a ripple effect. We are all one; nothing is separate; therefore, education will also reflect what we bring to it. This also is true for our environment; therefore, schools of the future will be high vibrational centers as the consciousness of humanity continues to rise. Rising was also reflected in being sovereign co-creators. What do we wish to create that will support us for the highest good of all? Also, what do we choose to de-create to allow more space for expansion?

Another theme is "life is school," as several authors have written directly in their stories. This in itself shows the expansion into the new paradigm of thinking! We have left behind the old paradigm, whereby learning happened only through third-dimensional aspects, such as testing, formalized classrooms, and set curricula, and have instead walked across a bridge of light towards fourth and fifth dimensions, where learning occurs through life experiences, heart-aligned visions, and multi-dimensional frequencies.

Key Wisdom Questions for *A New Paradigm of Education Rising*

Below are some thought-provoking questions the authors and I channeled to serve us all collectively. I encourage you to answer these questions after completing a meditation to allow for a more holistic response, where the hemispheres of the left and right brain are in alignment. It's not about getting the perfect answer but about applying your inner wisdom to open ideas that can later be expanded upon.

In our last book, *A New Paradigm of Education*, we also created key questions with the intent of being a bridge from the old paradigm way of thinking into the new method, some of which are included from number seven onwards. There are limitless solutions to these questions.

1. What are the key factors to consider for holistic education?

2. How can we bring more joy to ourselves, our students, and our children?

3. Life is school. How does this play out within your perspective of education?

4. How can we rise into sovereign mentors, students, and educators?

5. What are the fundamental values that will serve humanity throughout any paradigm shift?

6. What kinds of communication are in this new paradigm?

7. What's your experience with how students' learning can be supported using EQ or higher intelligence, rather than only IQ?

8. What would a world with limitless education look like?

9. What would education look like without a curriculum?

10. What's your vision for A New Paradigm of Education?

Closing Our Circle with Gratitude

The rainbow-flamed sunset danced across the sky as we sat in grace and reverence for all that was created in our circle meeting. We acknowledge our ancestors, light beings, family, animals, nature, children, and everyone who has taken a step toward creating a new paradigm and a new way on Earth that collectively serves us. The authors and I thank *you* for being part of this vortex of change with us. I thank our authors, Danielle, Alisha, Ida, Arianna, Meka, Heidi, Sian, Brittany, Janeen, Khiana, Aitabé, Karen, Julie, Clare, and myself for writing this book of light that serves the collective field of education. Finally, I acknowledge each of us for trusting our inner wisdom and visions about what a new paradigm of education means collectively.

As the stars shine luminously upon the resting sky, we are reminded to go within and assimilate the education received at this meeting. It's a moment to pause, but it's not the end of the ceremony, as *A New Paradigm of Education Rising* is constantly evolving. As we rise with the awakened sun, it's my vision that this book is not the end but the continuation of many more radical paradigm shifts within education.

We thank *you* for being a part of this journey into *A New Paradigm of Education Rising* with us and inspiring radical, heart-centered change for the greater good of humanity and future generations of change-makers rising into their greatness in all aspects of the mind, body, and soul as custodians of Earth and beyond. Thank you!

Go to: www.anewparadigmofeducation.com or www. moniquesayers.com/a-new-paradigm-of-education/

"The new paradigm creates unity, teaching the concept of oneness by illustrating our innate connection to each other and all species on Mother Earth."

~ Brittany Tackett

AUTHOR BIOGRAPHIES

Chapter One: Aitabé Fornés

Aitabé (Alison Fornés, M.Ed.) is the creator of *Sensethinking*. She is a Family and Systemic Constellations facilitator, a former NYC high school teacher, and a current unschooling mom.

She became fascinated with how the principles of Constellation work could be applied to education. Sensethinking is the result of her inquiry and dedication.

"This work is personal for me. I am the multiracial daughter of ancestors from all over the world, but I grew up with no connection to the language, culture, or places from which they came. It always seemed strange that I could be biologically made of these people and their stories yet not know how to connect with them. Family Constellations taught me how to make contact with my own lost stories."

"Through Constellation work, I started to discern a pattern about the nature of information that completely redefined how I understand the nature of learning. Sensethinking is the result of this new understanding. With Sensethinking, I teach everyone how to explore questions and lost stories that matter to them."

"One of the lessons of Sensethinking is that information has an energetic signature. We don't need to fear or be divided over information when we can identify the energetic signature of information aligned with the health and thriving of a system. This is the gift of Sensethinking."

You can reach Aitabé at sensethinking@gmail.com and visit her website https://www.sensethinking.com

Chapter Two: Brittany Tackett

Brittany Tackett, MA, is a transpersonal therapist, EQ coach, yoga and meditation teacher, homeschooling mom, and founder of HeartFirst Education, whose mission is to educate the whole person, heart first.

Brittany spent four academic years working as a school-based mental health therapist in public schools, where she supported more than 100 children and teens in developing self-regulation, coping skills, and stress resilience. She still works with children, but now, as an emotional intelligence (EQ) coach operating under a new lens. Rather than seeing suffering children as having a disorder that needs to be diagnosed and treated, she recognizes them as young humans struggling to cope in our messy world.

Brittany's goal as an EQ coach is to empower children with tools to regulate their nervous system and develop greater self-regulation, self-awareness, and self-esteem. She not only works with children one-on-one but offers group programs and courses, as well, through HeartFirst Kids, the world's first online social-emotional learning network for children.

Brittany also provides transpersonal therapy and coaching to women. Her signature program, Lean into Love, helps women get out of their heads and hearts through heart chakra yoga, meditation, shadow work, journaling, and sisterhood circles.

Brittany holds a Master of Arts in Transpersonal Psychology, a 200-hour yoga certification, Yoga for Emotional Intelligence certification, and an International Certificate in Applied Behavioral Studies.

Connect with Brittany:

Web:

www.heartfirsteducation.org

www.heartfirstkids.com

Email:

support@heartfirsteducation.org

Instagram:

@heartfirsteducation

@heartfulhomeschool

Chapter Three: Arianna Fox

Arianna Fox's ideas are revolutionary and wide-reaching, known across the region as a little ball of joy and energy. She has devoted her life to reaching out to others to spread messages of hope, inspiration, and self-confidence. Making a positive impact on others is part of this girlpreneur's goal.

With her motivational speaking style and ability to engage audiences of all ages, it's easy to understand how Arianna has raised her platform from her humble hometown in Delaware, USA to a vast network online.

This fifteen-year-old sensation is a national award winner with the acclaimed NFPW (National Federation of Press Women) and the DPA (Delaware Press Association). She's also a professional voiceover actress, performing for online commercial ads, web series, and commercials, such as Old Navy, Amazon, Taco Bell, Plato's Closet, Edible

Arrangements, Sky Zone, and more. She is bilingual and loves learning about languages and cultures and being a best-selling author and actress.

Arianna has been interviewed and featured by many media outlets, including Thrive Global, Medium.com/Authority Magazine, VoyageLA, DelmarvaLife/WBOC TV, and The Teen Magazine, and contributed multiple times to the nationally published K.I.S.H. Magazine. Arianna has been unstoppable since the age of six. Her first publication, *The Princess Chronicles*, was released in early 2017. Her second book is an Amazon best-selling novel titled *False Awakening*. Her third book, *Sabre Black*, is a fantasy/sci-fi young adult novel.

Watch out, world; here she comes!

"You Rock, Dream Big, and You Got This!"

Chapter Four: Julie Ferris

Julie is a #1 best-selling author of *Navigating Anxiety with Children and Teens, A Spiritual view of Anxiety* and self-published co-author of over 15 short stories that guide the reader through a gradual process of connecting with themselves, their souls, and our beautiful planet.

She works with parents and carers to deepen the connection with their children. Empowering others to realize they have the tools within to do this is close to her heart.

"It's my life's calling to support and empower people in the ways that I can. It's my passion to help highly sensitive, uniquely gifted children and young people. Those of us entrusted with their care to thrive in today's challenging world, and for all of us who are highly sensitive to realize and celebrate who we truly are so that we can reveal the remarkable gifts and talents that we all have inside of us." *Julie Ferris, Co-creator of The Gateway to The Avatar in You.*

Julie is mum to a uniquely gifted child, an intuitive guide, mindfulness instructor, quantum energy healer, and an intuitive artist. She has been a secondary school teacher and safeguarding professional within child protection in the police service and holds a degree in Psychology and a PGCE.

Julie loves to explore new places with her family and energetic puppy, particularly around Somerset and old Avalon, connecting deeply with nature and supporting her child's connection with sacred land.

Connect for a free discovery session to explore how they may support you and your family.

https://linktr.ee/julieferris

Chapter Four: Karen Goodson

Karen is a #1 best-selling author of *Navigating Anxiety with Children and Teens, A Spiritual view of Anxiety* (2022) and self-published co-author of over 15 short stories that guide the reader through a gradual process of connecting with themselves, their souls, and our beautiful planet.

She also contributed to *Co-Production in Mental Health: Not just another guide* (2018), a review of a ground-breaking project that enabled her to combine her passion for teaching with her lived experience of mental health.

Over the past 40 years, Karen has worked in care management, community arts, career advice, safeguarding and teaching vulnerable adults in the community. An award-winning tutor in Community Education for her innovative work with the Mental Health Recovery College, Karen lives her passion for revolutionizing the learning experience for her students.

Since her brother's suicide, Karen has developed a holistic approach to her work, blending spiritual counseling with quantum healing, channeling and coaching, and empowering people to reclaim their personal sovereignty.

Karen's lifelong dream has been to embrace a permaculture model of community with like-minded people, connecting deeply with the land, creating a space where those who share these values may visit, experience connection, and co-create New Earth. This dream is coming closer to reality on Karen's farm in Catalunya, Spain, currently unspoiled, thus providing a broad canvas for co-creating a New Paradigm of Education and Life.

The Portal of Potential

As co-creators of The Portal of Potential, Julie and Karen channeled the Avatar communication cards and many short stories, along with a unique spiritual development pathway to ascension. Julie specializes in delivering workshops for parents and loved ones who need support in parenting uniquely gifted children. Karen's focus is creating space for fellow healers and therapists to expand their work into the 5th dimension and beyond. Karen and Julie have an amazing gift for soul connection and communication, which brings about profound soul healing.

Julie and Karen offer a complimentary discovery session to explore how they may support you and your family.

https://linktr.ee/karengoodson

Ten Cloaks eBook https://bit.ly/3LbbsFc

The Choice – eBook https://bit.ly/3Q4aFa7

Chapter Five: Ida Rahayu

Ida Rahayu brings people back to Earth by reminding us that we are all part of the same ecosystem called "life." She shares her passion as a teacher at the renowned Green School in Bali, Indonesia and has used her position to take her Earth-based wisdom to local schools around the island.

Ida is the founder of the Cita Bumi Rahayu foundation and the Seeds to Table programs. This educational platform provides solutions to waste and invents smarter and healthier ways of producing and preparing food. She believes that education is the key to helping, especially students as our future generations, to impact the food they eat positively.

She plays her role as part of the big world to respect all other parts of the ecosystem (plants, animals, water, soil, microorganisms, fungi, air, etc.) and live in harmony with all of them. Ida hopes that what she does as an individual can inspire others. A good teacher doesn't teach; a good teacher inspires.

To reach Ida: idainbali@gmail.com or Seeds To Table In Bali (FB or IG)

Facebook:

https://www.facebook.com/ SeedstoTableinBali?mibextid=ZbWKwL

Instagram:

https://www.instagram.com/seedstotableinbali/

Chapter Six: Danielle Hayes

Danielle Hayes is the founder of *Calm Kids: Counselling & Wellbeing Service* - a holistic mental health support service for children and adolescents in Australia. She is also the co-founder of *Time For Change*, an educational well-being and consulting service in Bali, Indonesia.

After a 30-year career in education as a teacher, school counselor, and principal of a holistically based International School, Danielle felt that she needed to step out of the school system to advocate further for increased trauma awareness within schools and families. Danielle now works individually with children, adolescents, and families as a holistic counselor, providing time and a safe space for children and parents to explore their challenges and co-create their healing journey. She is fascinated by current research into Interpersonal Neurobiology and Polyvagal Theory and describes herself as an avid lifelong learner.

Danielle is deeply passionate about the mental health challenges educators and parents face. With her partner, Anthony, she presents engaging workshops to educators, parents, and community groups in Australia and internationally. Her workshop topics include: 'Conscious Parenting,' 'Parenting Your Anxious Child,' 'Calm Teachers - Calm Kids,' and 'Co-Regulation For Learning,' to name a few. Danielle is currently planning her first retreat for educators in Bali in 2023.

Danielle loves to travel the world, and she is inspired by her partner of 32 years and her two adult children, Caitlin and Connor. Danielle now divides her time between Australia and her 'soul home,' Bali.

To connect with Danielle and find out more about her services for families, children, and educators, please reach her at www. calmkidswellbeing.com.au or message her via Facebook/IG @calmkidsnow

Chapter Seven: Clare Ford

Clare Ford is a multi-award-winning academic coach with over 20 years of teaching experience, an international best-selling author, and the founder of Switched**ON!**, a cutting-edge global education platform offering inspirational education solutions.

She has spoken on numerous radio shows, Australian TV, international parenting and education summits, and podcasts about redefining education with her unique learning method that supports students.

After 12 years of ticking boxes and battling the old system in mainstream education, she burned out, becoming ill, anxious, and depressed. Clare stepped back from teaching, disillusioned, and trained as a Reiki Master, Quantum Energy Healer, and Parenting Coach. In 2016, she launched her well-being business and wrote her first book, *How to Have a Positive and Empowering Pregnancy.* Subsequently, Clare started the Mind, Baby Soul movement, running her first public event, "Loving Mothers."

In 2020, she was guided to reclaim the teaching space and launched "SwitchedON!" to support families with home education. Her online community, the Home Education Hub, provides a huge range of resources not just to educate but to empower and elevate. During the summer of 2020, Clare collaborated with children on another book, *Lollipops and Rainbows — Teaching Literacy with Soul.*

She is passionate about allowing families to learn in a way that unlocks their passions and allows the potential of every student to shine with courses in the classic, clever, and quantum curriculum in her unique online learning academy, SwitchedON!

You can contact Clare at link.ee/switchedonacademy1

Chapter Eight: Jeneen Gacek

Jeneen Gacek, a multi-passionate entrepreneur, a Mindful Parenting Guide, and a Self-Directed Learning Facilitator, helps parents awaken to and zone in on a New Path for Parenting and Learning.

Jeneen comes from a business marketing background with multiple businesses but has landed on her Personal Passion Project after experiencing self-directed learning with her family. Her world is woven together by an intercultural marriage, two teenagers, and living in a foreign country, Bali, Indonesia.

Jensen's company, Remindful Life, is a platform for intentional living, focusing on interactive, playful ways for families looking to thrive individually and as a family unit. Remindful Life has been featured on multiple platforms and podcasts, including Global Nomad Parents, Building Heroes, and Our Year in Bali Community. In addition, Jeneen has organized World Cafe Events for Community Conversation and Self-Directed Teen Workshops to explore creativity and give teens a feeling of choice.

Jeneen is President of the Canggu, Bali Toastmasters International Club and supports the community in speaking their ideas and finding their authentic voices. She studied at the Graduate Institute for Transformative Learning and Antioch University, specializing in Experiential Consciousness.

Jeneen's true passion and North Star foster and develop human flourishing through Self-Awareness, Flow, Self-Directed Learning, Project Based Learning, and Personalization over Standardization.

Sign up now to explore the New Paradigm of Parenting and find ways to thrive as a family. Website: www.remindfullife.com

Chapter Nine: Khiana Kalli Gacek

Khiana Kalli Gacek is 15 years old and raised on the island of Bali. She often walks barefoot, stating, "Shoes are cages for the feet." Because she values freedom and self-expression, she is open to new opinions but unapologetically shares her own. Being respectfully honest with a bizarre, witty side characterizes her views on life. She loves long walks on the beach and honors feet from all walks of life.

Her family supports her self-directed learning journey, her mom, a co-author in the book, and her father, a creative designer, and her older brother. With a family that values curiosity, humor, and self-expression, thinking outside the box is second nature.

Her interests run broad but originated from Beauty and Special Effects Makeup. She designed and created a full-body Yeti costume consisting of hand-molded teeth, facial prosthetics and sculpted horns, and an elaborate devil costume for a performance art exhibition. In addition, she had independent contracts for weekly events, parties, concerts, and photo shoots.

Khiana's final project culmination was a 100-Day Makeup challenge, where she conceptualized, designed, and created 100 different makeup looks including blood and gore, illusion art, and creature creation. These projects inspired her to dive more creatively into film, art, music, writing, and history. As a result, she dabbled in fashion history, music composition, sculpting, photography, and script writing. In contrast to her creative interests lies a deep fascination and curiosity for the world and how things work. This led to her interest in chemistry, philosophy, and travel.

She aspires to create, express, and 'think outside the shoe.'

Chapter Ten: Alisha Braché

Alisha Braché is the creator of Cosmic Gateway and New Earth Children. As an Intuitive, Soul Reader, Writer, Energy Practitioner & Teacher, she has dedicated her life from a young age to her soul's path. Working with refining her Psychic, Intuitive & Healing Abilities to work and support others in finding their path and deeper understanding of their soul's journey.

Over 20 years of formal studies and practice have developed her intuitive and healing gifts. Trained in all forms of esoteric and energy techniques (Psychic Mediumship, Trance/ Channeling, Energy Healing, Past Life Regression, Reiki, Quantum Healing & many more.)

She continued into a more Holistic Healing approach and studied as a Holistic Living Counselor. Since working with clients, Alisha's work has transitioned over the years to focus on supporting children and parents to understand better sensitivity and special and unique abilities from a soul-centered holistic perspective.

Alisha works with a wide range of energy techniques and modalities influenced by her cosmic origins and star family to bring forth a range of advanced techniques to support people through Ascension, retrieving soul memory and lost aspects, healing traumas through the multidimensional field, and humanity towards a New Earth reality.

Alisha's gifts spring from the wealth of her unique life experiences involving lifelong contact and connection to the Spirit and Cosmic realms. In addition, Alisha's unique experiences have given her the ability to work with those she supports in unique spiritual gifts and New Earth Children.

Alisha's website links:

www.cosmicg8way.com

www.newearthchildren.org

Chapter Eleven: Heidi Conway

Heidi Conway, an international trainer of life coaches, national health and safety manager in the corporate world with an Environmental Science degree in her past, and today, she is an on-purpose Aussie mother of two home-educated teens, living her passion raising them as the changemakers they were born to be. Heidi has been reviewed as being able to converse with your mind while listening to your soul. It makes sense, then, that Heidi would listen to her sons and know that, in the traditional school environment, their inner genius she heard and saw often was not sustainably lit. They learned differently. This had repercussions in the classroom and she was eventually told one was not writing and the other was not focusing.

Heidi is now on a global mission to reduce the pain in the world by allowing young people to be their true selves. Heidi is CEO and the edupreneur of Changemaker Teens Global, a movement that is revolutionizing the outdated, unresponsive traditional education system; she is redefining school for teens with authentic alternative education. Much to the delight of once tired and frustrated mothers, the real learning that takes place in her *'Raising Changemakers Mastermind™'* is transforming teens refusing to learn and showing signs of apathy, deception, rejection, attrition, confusion, and boredom, into joyful teens now prepared for the future, focused, connected, and engaging in their choices, interests, passion, and their purpose with ease, the changemaker way.

At the same time, mothers and mentors are invited to be the catalyst for this positive change as they confidently learn how to be the change and raise changemaker teens, holding space for the transformation to discover and embrace who they are, how they know, find their unique passion, take inspired action, and align to living a life of purpose and meaning.

To reach Heidi:

www.changemakerteens.global

www.facebook.com/groups/raisingchangemakerteens

Chapter Twelve: Sian Goodspeed

Sian Goodspeed is a home-educating mother of two daughters, an experienced teacher, and the founder of two education companies. Sian was a primary school teacher for twelve years before leaving the classroom in 2009 to set up Flying Start Tuition. This award-winning tuition company combines Neuro-Linguistic Programming (NLP) techniques with more traditional teaching methods. The emphasis is on helping students to develop a positive attitude to learning, boosting confidence, self-motivation, and independence, enabling them to learn and progress more effectively.

In 2021, inspired by her training in Nonviolent Communication (NVC), Sian launched Be more giraffe. Sian believes that compassionate connection is the key to healing the world and the power to do so lies within every one of us. She is passionate about helping others to unlock that power, and her 'Be more giraffe' workshops aim to do just that.

Using the engaging and memorable metaphors of the giraffe and the jackal, Sian teaches the nonviolent communication process, along with tools and techniques designed to foster greater empathy for others and ourselves.

Sian hopes that, by bringing her experience of NVC to others in a fun and easy-to-grasp way, they may be inspired to join her in her quest to live a more harmonious, happy, and fulfilling life.

"Imagine a world where we all view each other through compassion rather than judgment... and imagine viewing yourself through that same lens...That's the world I want to live in." Sian Goodspeed

Email: hello@bemoregiraffe.com

Website: www.bemoregiraffe.com

Website: www.flyingstarttuition.co.uk

Chapter Thirteen: Meka Leach

National traveling yoga teacher Meka Leach is 13 years old and from the USA. She is a certified Bhakti yoga teacher of 200 hours, the youngest in the USA to finish the certification classes. In addition, she is a certified Harmonic Waves Healing practitioner, performing sound healing for adult-only as well as children-only classes.

Meka is the youngest instructor and facilitator at the Soderworld wellness center and the surrounding area/ community. Meka is the founder of *Mindfulness with Meka,* a class and program for all ages. She creates handwritten workbooks from her soul for each class for her students to take home and continue their mindful journey.

At ten, Meka started teaching a kids-only class about conscious living, breathwork, meditation, and self-love. She is an amazing, loving soul, passionate about holistic health and mindful practice. She is a Reiki Master. She loves crystals, and Meka wants to change her generation.

She has been featured in Yoga Chicago and seen on many news channels as an uplifting story https://yogachicago. com/2019/10/meka-leach-yoga-teacher-and-sound-healer-at-age-10/.

You can reach Meka at mindfulnesswithmeka@gmail.com

Follow her on Facebook and Instagram Mindfulnesswithmeka

Chapter Fourteen : Monique Sayers

Monique Sayers is a mother, educator, light worker, author, and visionary of *A New Paradigm of Education*. This mission was birthed to support the children and adult change-makers in the rise of consciousness on Earth that we are all co-creating. It has inspired the co-creation of two books within the International Best-selling series, *A New Paradigm of Education*. She has also connected with many souls on the same mission to evolve the consciousness of education through the podcast *A New Paradigm of Education*. It's a rise-to-root approach, meaning first, Monique will visualize in the Quantum and then bring forth soul-aligned pieces that will serve the mission. More to come!

Monique was born in Australia but has spent most of her life traveling and living abroad. She's taught over 20,000 students from around the world TEFL/English, Primary School, and 1-1 classes. She's physically taught in China, Bali, Uruguay, and Australia. Her favorite classroom is the ocean, and her greatest teacher is her daughter, Coral.

Monique is a blessing giver, meditation guide, Ekam Mitra, Quantum Practitioner, and student of the light. She shares some of her wisdom in *A Journey of Riches-The Attitude of Gratitude,* which is an International Best-selling co-authored book. In addition, Monique offers a range of energy sessions, guided meditations, and Quantum sessions for adults and children.

Monique would love to support your children with one-on-one or small group sessions in foundational skills, English, meditation, Quantum, and other new paradigm ways of learning. All her work is done intuitively as she co-creates with children in a fun and unique way. She also offers guided meditation and personalized sessions in the Quantum for healing, upgrading and expansion for adults individually or with your children as well.

Email: anewparadigmofeducation@gmail.com

Follow Us: A New Paradigm of Education/ Monique Coral

Websites: www.moniquesayers.com or https://www.anewparadigmofeducation.com/

"We are grateful to have traveled onto the bridge of light *A New Paradigm of Education Rising,* and beyond with you, our ancestors, and future generations of change-makers, creating a collective vision together. Now let us all soar and *rise* sovereignly, in connection, choosing the highest frequency of love. This is education. And so it is."

~Monique Sayers

Amazon Reviews for the International Best-selling series *A New Paradigm of Education*

An awesome and inspiring Read

I was so excited when I came across *A New Paradigm of Education*, written and compiled by Monique Sayers. This book is a book for its time, which is now. My opinion is there is very little heart left in education, which is very sad, because Primary school children really need this. I think *A New Paradigm of Education* is extremely relevant and actually brilliant. It gives me hope we can somehow, in the future, support young people to follow their hearts and dreams.

~ Brandon Giffard

Great book for all educators and parents to read!

As a teacher of over 30 years, it is great to see a book about creativity, growth, and how to let all children be the "best that they can be" in their own eyes. Wonderful reading and highly recommended to all educators and parents!

~ Randy S

This book has revolutionized my thinking

I love this book so much. As a teacher, this book was for my soul. So many days, I work to compensate for a system that is failing so many of our babies, and reading this book gave me more organized thinking and steps to implement strategies to take my teaching to the next level. Also, as a parent of four, it also is helpful for us to learn different ways to reach our kids. We may think that they are struggling with school, but you will find from this book that it's the schools learning strategies that are the problem.

Great book, great subject. Can't wait for more workbooks about education.

~ Saantis Davis

This book is a game changer!

A New Paradigm of Education is a game-changer in the world of education. Our kids have evolved, and we need their education to reflect this. The book gives tangible tips to begin cultivating a new way of educating and connecting with the next generation.

~ Amazon Customer

Manufactured by Amazon.ca
Bolton, ON

31739856R00173